Kultermann   New Architecture in the World

Udo Kultermann

New
Architecture
in the World

 Universe Books, Inc., New York

Translated from the German by Ernst Flesch

First printing
published in the United States of America
by Universe Books, Inc.
381 Park Avenue South
New York, N. Y. 10016

Library of Congress Catalog Card Number: 65–24565
© Verlag Wasmuth, Tübingen 1965

Printed in Germany

CONTENTS

INTRODUCTION

While, formerly, there existed such fundamental differences in style as the clay architecture of Central Africa and Chinese wooden edifices that they could not possibly be considered as comparable forms of artistic expression, the criteria of international architecture are today applicable everywhere.

However, the tasks which face both architects and others with ever-increasing urgency, remain unsolved. In fact, only a small part of the most pressing problems is now being recognized as such for the first time. Contemporary architecture is thus in the midst of a crisis. The problems requiring urgent solution and the possibilities of finding proper solutions are not reconcilable· Not only architecture is today in a state of crisis but also human society as a whole. This forces one to attempt a discussion and clarification of fundamental principles in order to be in a position to recognize clearly the present tasks and the requirements of the community. In many instances the tasks confronting architecture are not stated specifically. They are not clearly defined and consequently do not lead to common efforts directed towards a solution. No generally held conception of value exists as to what contemporary architecture is or ought to be.

The architect himself, in his work, frequently touches only the fringe of the problems which he should examine, define and solve from a fundamental point of view. The question is whether he will continue to be content with bearing only a fraction of the responsibility for the important new developments. He will have to strive, not only for that greater synthesis to which his own individual creative efforts, within the context of town and regional planning, communications and industrialization, are contributing, but also, above all, for greater diversity.

The general attitude in relation to tradition has in consequence also entered into a crisis, for tradition can at all times only arise out of creative effort and therefore appears new at every stage of development. Thus, even the works of the classic Mies van der Rohe, Le Corbusier and Gropius have been questioned critically. They have now gained the same level as the works of bygone centuries and, being part of existing monuments, form the general consciousness of our time. And yet they must be continuously questioned and viewed afresh if they are to be of value to us in their embodiment of the living past.

The architecture of the present day has been given many names with which an attempt was made to define, in retrospect, certain tendencies of development. These concepts can either seek a connection with the names of past styles or point to the future, namely in the case when they strive to characterize a certain new line of endeavor. Thus, on the one hand, the concepts "Neo-Classicism," "Neo-Liberty" or "Neo-Empirism" represent attempts to establish a direct link with styles of the past, and are indeed conscious efforts to return, in an academic sense, to certain achievements of the past in order to make use of them; (in the case of the term "Neo-Neoplasticism" such an attempt at definition actually leads to a potential assimilation of style). On the other hand, definitions arising out of certain characteristics of individual buildings or out of the requests of individual architects, such as the terms "Brutalism," "Dynamism," "Metabolism," "Mobile Architecture," "Chemical Architecture," or "Absolute Architecture" are seeking either for the purpose of a manifest or simply by means of factual descriptions, to define in a meaningful form the characteristic features of the new.

"Brutalism," for example, developed in contradistinction to the refined tradition of the work of Mies van der Rohe, whose style formed the starting-point for the work of most important representatives of this tendency, Peter and Alison Smithson. Rayner Banham characterized these endeavors as follows: "The fundamental aim of 'Brutalism' was at all times to find a conception which, from the point of view of construction, space, organization and materials, represents what is 'necessary,' in the Smithsonian sense, for a certain building." The aim was no longer to conceal the structural forms and installations, but on the contrary to express visibly how something is made.

The term "Asceticism," based on the example of the work of a few Scandinavian architects, came into existence in a similar way. Here, too, architecture has been reduced to only the most essential elements. This definition has an exclusive meaning, i. e. it stands in contrast to something else. The Asceticists avoid certain common forms, and by cutting down the means employed, arrive at that clarity of architectural expression which they consider essential.

Concepts such as "Action Architecture," "Dynamism," "Mobile Architecture" or "Metabolism" are based on the condition of change and acceleration indispensable for us as well as on a new conception of space and demand – in the main logically, on an urbanist basis – the recognition and solution of new problems. Movement and change, continuity and variability, as well as totally new technical possibilities all play a part in this. The traditional conception of architecture is extended

tremendously in the theory and practice of these young architects.

Which of the buildings belonging to the immediate present (as distinct from those of previous decades), give an indication of these changed directions of development? Where lies that creative continuity of tradition which at any given moment is only possible when seen in relation to contemporary needs? What shifts of emphasis have taken place in the international scene? What new tasks exist in China, India, Africa and South America and what part is being played by countries such as Israel, Japan, Yugoslavia, Hungary or Rumania? In which countries are possibilities created by present-day industrial conditions being transformed into practice, and where do obstructionist tendencies directed towards a sterile incorporation of traditional forms prevent the course of progress?

These questions – and in many cases they will remain questions – will be pursued in this book. The answers are being supplied in practice by the architects themselves, but not by them alone, for every new building is the result of society coming to terms with the challenges confronting it, and shows the ability of this society to deal with these in its own way.

It is necessary today to form a judgment of the total structure of contemporary world architecture. There are no longer any achievements which can be seen in isolation. Continuing the work begun in the volume "Architecture of Today" (New York 1959) the task of the present book is to examine questions concerned with a world-wide architecture. The realities of the year 1965 demand a new presentation taking into account developments since 1959 and the shifts of emphasis in the international situation. Even more compellingly than in 1959 we feel, today, the world-wide interconnections, from which nothing can any longer be isolated, within which every part is inextricably interwoven with all the others. Architects more than ever before will have to look beyond the frontiers of their own countries – not only in order to receive stimulation, but in order to comprehend their common task. A universal sense of interconnection is today both a reality and a necessity.

BUILDINGS FOR STATE AND MUNICIPAL ADMINISTRATION

In contrast to bygone centuries our time has seldom succeeded in giving architectural expression to the feelings of a community. Thus the buildings of the supernational organizations, government buildings, and the administrative centers of smaller communities are in most cases "official architecture."

Throughout the world there exist only a few exceptions where the task and its realization are suitably related. Within the framework of Lúcio Costa's plan for the new capital city of Brasília, the central government buildings by Oscar Niemeyer dominate, symbolizing the three divisions of power in the state, but these edifices are not free from elements of ostentation as we have known in the past. The Congress building with two office towers and two assembly halls, the Supreme Court and the residence of the President lie at the intersection of the residential and business areas which are arranged in a wing-shaped pattern and they crown the central administrative axis of the city.

Le Corbusier, too, created an administrative center within the framework of the new capital of the Punjab, Chandigarh. He built the Capitol which is detached from the general structure of the town and which combines the Supreme Court, the Secretariat and the Parliament. The building for the Chamber of Deputies and the Upper House, completed last, was designed to stand out from the previously built sections of the Capitol by means of its plastic form. The architect clearly envisaged it as the central focal point of the community, in this case of a province, and designed it accordingly, although in the long run it will certainly not be sufficient for the requirements of the growing city organism.

Pakistan also, after the partition of the former Indian Colonial Empire, had need of a new capital in the western part of the country, and therefore founded the city of Islamabad. Several villages were amalgamated for this purpose. For the central parliament building to be included in the overall plan by Constantinos A. Doxiadis various designs were submitted. Arne Jacobsen envisaged a cylindrical parliament hall projecting from a horizontal base tract planned to serve as a platform, inside which the administration offices would be situated. Raglan Squires in his design created a structure composed of open and closed spaces for the various subsidiary buildings, crowned by the cupola of the central parliament hall. As not only the President's and Prime Minister's residences but whole residential areas were included in the plan, it is here, in contrast to Chandigarh, not a matter of a purely administrative district, but of a combination of various constructional tasks. In addition, there was a conscious attempt to base the style on Mogul architectural forms.

Satisfactory solutions to the problems of the construction of city halls have been found both in Japan and in Europe in recent years. The buildings by Alvar Aalto for Säynätsalo in 1951, those by Arne Jacobsen for various Danish cities and by Kenzo Tange for some smaller Japanese towns decided the architectural forms in many cases. New paths emerged from the competition held in 1958 for the design of Toronto City Hall, which attracted exciting contributions from many countries, so that the publication of the competition result itself acted as a stimulus for the development of international architecture. Of extraordinary significance was the fact that the superb design by the Finnish architect Viljo Revell was accepted and construction was completed in 1965. It consists of two office towers of unequal height arranged elliptically, with curved groundplans, of which the walls have a convex shape towards the outside and of a low central assembly hall, enclosed by these two curved towers. The whole complex lies on a raised ground plateau, which contains both the approach roads and the necessary installations. The general form of the construction distinguishes this administrative center from the prevailing styles of multi-storied buildings.

Louis I., Kahn, as early as in 1952/3 and in 1957 created designs for city halls which are similarly characterized by the inclusion of a tower growing out of a flat base, accentuating the normal aspect of the town. These designs have not been carried out, but Kahn did get the opportunity to complete the considerably less complicated city hall in Bristol, Pennsylvania, in which, as distinct from the early designs partially influenced by

Richard Buckminster Fuller, classicist forms play a certain part.

The Danish architect Arne Jacobsen in his halls, such as the beautiful building in Rødovre (1955) or in Glostrup (1958) continues the tradition of Mies van der Rohe. Jacobsen's design of 1962 for the Essen City Hall also remains within the limits of this tradition. Another Danish city hall construction was carried out by the architects Halldor Gunlogsson and Jørn Nielsen in 1959 in Tarnby, a district of Copenhagen. K. Lund and N. Slaato erected an unpretentious building in Asker near Oslo. By means of a strictly horizontal arrangement these young architects succeeded in creating a harmonious whole, consisting of an office tower and communal installations of low elevation. The attractive interplay of glass and rough concrete lends the construction its special character.

The Dutch architects van den Broek and Bakema found a different form of solution for this building task in the town hall of Marl. This center for a small industrial community created a stir with its hanging office towers and the use of rough concrete.

An extraordinary degree of maturity is shown in the new town halls in Japan. Here the task has found its own special expression as a result of the new relationship between the individual and the community. It has, in fact, been modified to such an extent that in many cases it is possible to talk of a community center rather than a town hall, as various functions have frequently been combined in this type of building. The development of the modern town hall in Japan must therefore be seen as representing a fundamental transformation extending right down to individual details.

Kunio Mayekawa designed edifices for various town centers in Tokyo. Junzo Sakakura built the town hall in Hajima in the prefecture of Gifu; Kenji Imai, that of Otakimachi. Takeo Sato erected the town halls of Niigata, Iwakuni, Asahikawa, Bunkyo-Ku and Kokura.

Of the greatest significance, however, is the work of Kenzo Tange, whose town hall constructions represent the various stages of the new Japanese architecture. The great administrative center of the metropolis of Tokyo, while its final form was not quite in accordance with Tange's designs, is an important achievement of post-war Japanese architecture. The town hall of Shimizu, of an earlier date, already consisted of two distinct parts, an office tower and a horizontal tract giving access to the public. This style reached it highest form in Takamatsu in the prefecture of Kagawa. Tange succeeded in creating a style of a different character in the city hall of his home town of Imabari, which together with the assembly hall, also designed by him, formed a center for the whole community. After completing the town hall of Kurayoshi on a smaller scale, Tange achieved an even more convincing synthesis in that of Kurashiki. In his designs for city halls he has attempted to overcome the traditional barriers between the Japanese public and the bureaucracy, and at the same time to give architectural expression to the communal spirit of the Japanese urban population.

A fascinating city hall construction was created at Bat Yam in Israel by the architects Neumann, Hecker and Sharon. Bat Yam is a small industrial town on the Mediterranean coast with a population of about 60,000. The square-shaped project of the town hall, with its upper stories jutting out in the form of an inverted pyramid, is part of a wider town plan constructed on different ground levels, which also includes shops, offices, a communal building and a link with the sea for pedestrian use. The individual shapes of the town hall, developing out of the basic quadratic form, and the monumental roof constructions lend the building its unique character. It has frequently been compared with the traditional Israeli form of the Ziggurat, of which an inverted version has been used here.

COMMUNAL BUILDINGS

Social development during the last few years has led increasingly to the creation of centers with varied, mostly cultural, functions. This applies to smaller towns as well as to districts in large cities. Frequently a cultural center of this sort is connected with the town hall. Possibilities exist, however, of linking them with assembly halls, churches, schools or even with shopping centers. Accommodation for lectures, concerts, film and theatrical performances, sports and games can, in fact, be linked with various constructional projects.

Such community centers usually consist of a large hall and a number of smaller groups of rooms and foyers. Outstanding examples in this field are the festival halls by Kunio Mayekawa in Kyoto and Tokyo. A large hall forms the center and all the other installations are grouped around this central function.

Hideo Kosaka created a comprehensive community center in Nagoya. In one great complex he combined a large auditorium, a central library, a museum, conference halls and a public restaurant, to serve the population of the entire prefecture. Kenzo Tange achieved a convincing architectural solution for the cultural center of the little town of Nichinan.

It is now several years since Walter Gropius, with his team "TAC," designed a large community center for the town of Tallahassee, Florida, a construction of dynamic shape which clearly distinguishes it from all the town's other public edifices as well as from the private houses. Unfortunately, this project has not been carried out.

Impressive complexes of buildings for congresses and other large-scale functions have been built in the Kremlin in Moscow, in Kyoto (by Sachio Ohtani), in Bucharest (by H. Maicu, T. Ricci, and I. Serban), Berlin and Peking. Alvar Aalto constructed a whole series of special cultural centers which include one in Helsinki in 1958 and a smaller building in Wolfsburg. American designs and models such as one by the young architect Martin Price, who, in a most convincing fashion, managed to link sports installations, a library, a concert hall, and a restaurant situated on different levels in such a way that the spaces between the individual buildings could be utilized for further functions including dances, discussions, talks and games, have remained on the drawing boards. The idea for a cultural center in Léopoldville in the Congo, by Takamasa Yoshizaka has also remained in the design stage.

MUSEUMS

The function of the museum in society has not yet been sufficiently defined. It is true that museum buildings were erected in numerous countries after the war, and yet such a fundamental conception, for example, as Le Corbusier's continuously growing museum has never materialized anywhere. There were solutions attempting to reach new forms based on the tasks set by contemporary art. In these it was necessary again and again to return to the aims of the Museum of Modern Art in New York as well as to the example of Le Corbusier, the creator of the museums of Tokyo and Ahmedabad, in India. The Museum of Western Art in Tokyo was intended to house a previously private collection of modern art. It was completed by the Japanese architects Mayekawa, Yoshizaka and Sakakura acording to Le Corbusier's designs. A very much more simple effect is created by the Ahmedabad building, also based on a square plan and standing on pillars, with its outer structure determined by ordinary brickwork. The mu-

seum is especially intended for evening visits and has a roof terrace with dense vegetation and numerous fountain basins.

In the Museum of Modern Art in Rio de Janeiro Affonso Eduardo Reidy, by using spatial structures detached from the ground, created an ensemble by loosely connecting various complexes of buildings. Its arrangement is on different levels, skillfully bridged by ramps of spacious proportions. As with all the important museum constructions of recent years the significance here is not confined to the setting up of art exhibitions and the building of a collection but, on the contrary, the museum's scope has been purposely extended into other fields; a school, lecture and work rooms, a theatre to hold a thousand spectators as well as rooms for concerts, ballet and film performances were incorporated into the ensemble.

The museum building in Turin by the architects Bassi and Boschetti is also dedicated to contemporary art. The Museum of the Twentieth Century in Vienna, which grew out of the Austrian Pavilion of the 1958 Brussels

World Fair, and the museum project of 1963 by the Yugoslav architect Vjenceslav Richter are based on the square design determined by Le Corbusier. The new building at Le Havre by Lagneau and Audigier, erected in cooperation with the civil engineer René Sarger, offers the greatest possible flexibility in the use of the existing space.

Striking designs for American museums have been made by I. M. Pei and Hanford Yang. Louis I. Kahn is responsible for the gallery of Yale University. Philip Johnson erected various museums in Utica, New York, in Fort Worth, Texas, and in Lincoln, Nebraska. Johnson, in his museum buildings, has abandoned the style of Mies van der Rohe, on which he modelled himself, and has followed Classicist tendencies. The gallery of the Munson Williams Proctor Institute in Utica, New York, built in the years 1957/60, is again based on a square-shaped plan, and being completely closed towards the outside, is lit entirely from above. The museum in San Salvador was built by the architects Katstaller and Schott, and in Jerusalem A. Mansfeld and Dora Gad erected a building on a number of different levels as a continuously growing museum.

Mies van der Rohe also had the opportunity of designing some museum constructions. He built a wing for the Art Museum in Houston, Texas, completed in 1958/59. The design for the Gallery of the Twentieth Century in Berlin is based on this prototype of a large open hall which can serve the most varied purposes.

Among German museum buildings the Lehmbruck Museum in Duisburg, by Manfred Lehmbruck, and the Folkwang Museum in Essen deserve special mention. In Scandinavia the additions to the Louisiana Museum near Copenhagen, by Bo and Wohlert are particularly successful.

THEATRES AND CONCERT HALLS

As is the case in so many other fields of construction, modern theatre building remains within the limits prescribed in the Twenties; it can indeed be said that significant projects such as that for a globe-shaped theatre by Weininger or the Total Theatre by Walter Gropius have, until now, not been realized. New buildings do exist in various towns of America, Australia, Asia and Europe, but the most important results include designs for smaller theatres or for purely experimental theatres.

Mies van der Rohe is responsible for the grandiose project designed in 1953 for the National Theatre in Mannheim, which was, however, never carried out. Its place was taken by a convincing work of Gerhard Weber. Two houses were linked together. In the smaller of these houses forms of the "Variable Theatre" can already be practiced, although the seats in the stalls are still fixed in place.

Other German theatre buildings came into existence in Hamburg, Münster, Gelsenkirchen and Bonn. Werner Ruhnau, in his design for a mobile theatre, went a step beyond the stage reached at Gelsenkirchen and, together with Emanuel Lindner and the French director Jacques Polieri, worked out a corresponding sketch for the competition for the Düsseldorf theatre. The larger and the smaller building were to be linked together without restrictions, this being achieved by making the entire floor area variable.

The most significant edifice of all was erected by Jørn Utzon for the city of Sidney; this is a powerful shell construction which forms the roof of two buildings. Here the intention is to create a cultural center in the broadest sense, extending far beyond the actual stage events. Thus, an experimental theatre, a school of dramatic art, a hall for chamber music recitals and a restaurant were incorporated into the complex.

Studios which represent an attempt to enliven the methods of theatre construction previously marked by their sterility, in order to make the creation of a theatre in the true contemporary sense possible, have come into being in Washington, D. C., built by Harry Weese, in Accra, Ghana, built by Gerlach and Gillies-Reyburn, in Chichester, England, by Powell and Moya, and in Mamaia, Rumania, by Cezar Lazarescu and the Iscas. The summer theatre in Mamaia, completed in 1963 and situated directly on the shore of the Black Sea, creates a free zone for a play no longer confined to any set limits. Noriaki Kurokawa designed an open-air theatre forming part of a children's camping ground. Frei Otto originated the design for an open-air theatre in Wunsiedel (1960/63) with a skin-like roof held up by poles and stretched by means of ropes covering the spectators' terraces.

It is not surprising that the construction of cinema buildings has seldom found an architecturally attractive form. In this field three edifices, all in Eastern Europe, have been included, namely the Köbánya Cinema in Budapest, built in 1963/64 by the architect Peter Molnár, the First of May Cinema in Bucharest, by G. Mularidis and Y. Goldenberg and the movie house "Kosmos" in East Berlin by Josef Kaiser.

In the field of concert hall construction the main attention is focused on the "Berlin Philharmonie" building erected in the years 1960/63 by Hans Scharoun. The form of this edifice was determined mainly by the acoustic requirements of its interior. It belongs to the expressionistic tradition of Scharoun's early work. The Gumma Music Center in Takasaki, a late work by Antonin Raymond, erected in 1958/61, is comparable to the "Berlin Philharmonie," although it stems from an entirely different tradition. The building can be used not only as a concert hall, but also for the staging of Kabuki theatre performances.

In addition to the above, buildings for broadcasting occupy an important place with this genre, for here also the acoustic aspects are decisive.

Among the most interesting recent attempts in this field is the tribune for choral singing in Vilno in the Lithuanian Soviet Republic, by Kotli, Sepman and Gelnus and the civil engineer Paalman. A similar covered tribune of light-weight construction was built in 1959 in Melbourne.

CHURCHES

Although, within the framework of present-day architectural tasks, church building and the construction of temples and monasteries no longer occupy the decisive position held in former times, a large number of churches have, nevertheless, come into being since the last war, with important architects furnishing the designs for some of them.

In a few countries attempts were made to incorporate additional functions in church constructions and to create communal centers. There were also spectacular events such as the erection of the pilgrimage church at Ronchamp by Le Corbusier or the competition designs for Syracuse.

In spite of the existence of numerous new church buildings in Northern Europe, in Scandinavia, England and Germany, the stress in this field can be said to lie above all in the Southern European area and Latin America. In these countries solutions of far-reaching significance have occasionally been achieved, as for example, the splendid Chapel of San Vincente de Paul in Coyoacan in Mexico, by the architects Enrique de la Mora and Fernando Lopez Carmona and the civil engineer Felix Candela. In this case they succeeded, by means of the roof form, in effectively symbolizing the function of the building. Other church constructions by Felix Candela also do this successfully, so that it is possible to describe Mexico as one of the few areas with a new religious architecture.

In South America attention must be drawn above all to the various edifices and projects of Oscar Niemeyer, who, right up to his work on the cathedral of the new capital of Brasília, has again and again occupied himself with ecclesiastical building problems.

Dynamic spaces and integration of color, light and volume, characterize the church designs of Enrico Castiglioni, which for the most part have not been carried out. Castiglioni succeeds in creating the essential unity of the various effective elements.

Other individual churches in various countries are convincing examples of contemporary architecture, as for instance the chapel in Tampere built by Viljo Revell in 1960, with its large parabolic form set opposite and in contrast to a horizontal tract lying in the forest. Eero Saarinen's chapel in Fort Wayne, Indiana, the chapel of Tunghai University near Tai Chung on Formosa by the Chinese architect Ieoh Ming Pei, as well as Kenzo

Tange's Tokyo Cathedral completed in 1964, are remarkable for their mighty tent-like silhouettes.

In church architecture, too, attempts have been made to find new paths by the use of site-assembling processes. Thus, Eckhard Schulze-Fielitz in his prefabricated chapel in Düsseldorf-Eller employed constructional forms which otherwise are principally used for exhibition buildings. In addition, some churches in Switzerland by Ernst Gisel, church buildings in Italy by Giovanni Micheluzzi and the church at Royan, France, by G. Gillet, are notable.

To what extent church construction has been adapted, or can be adapted, to the conditions of our age is not certain. In Switzerland projects exist for a Catholic church on the top floor of a residential building, in Japan there are temples which are also used as kindergartens, so that the church area has become a multi-purpose institution.

CLUB HOUSES AND HOSTELS

Youth hostels, kindergartens and children's homes, recreational institutions belonging to certain organizations or enterprises, and club buildings are mostly placed in beautiful scenic surroundings. For the architect it is a matter of making it possible for a usually temporary stay in a community to be passed in a pleasant way.

The Young Pioneers' camp in the Crimea, with its dormitory buildings integrated in the beautiful coastal landscape, and its open room areas connected by ramps is a good example of a recreational complex created by the use of contemporary architectural methods.

Aldo van Eyck, in his Children's House, in Amsterdam, proceeded in quite a different manner and created, logically, a precinct cut off to a great extent from its city surroundings. This complex characterized in its interior by rooms, paths and roads of varied sizes as well as by many installations adapted to children's perceptive capacity, represents an ideal residential environment for children.

The kindergarten in Lourenco Marques in Mozambique, by Amancio d'Alpoim Guedes, because of its clear-cut yet imaginative combination of closed and open spaces, is a children's kingdom all to itself.

Yoshinobu Ashihara, in the Youth Hostel in Nikko, created a crystalline domestic building for the accommodation of young people placed so as to contrast with the landscape.

The task of constructing communal buildings for certain professional organizations or larger enterprises follows different aims. More and more the trend today is towards shaping the nature of the leisure time and rest periods of the members of the staffs. On the one hand, communal recreation rooms can be accommodated in the upper floors of high buildings; on the other, in edifices specially constructed for the purpose. An automobile factory in Barcelona, for example, had recreation rooms erected in this way by the architects Cesar Ortiz de Echague, Raphael de la Joya and Manuel Barbero Rebolledo. A number of pavillion-like buildings of aluminum interspersed with garden spaces form an attractive recreational center. Rather similar is the Nishijin Labor Center in Kyoto by Noriaki Kurokawa, which is also used for further education. Similar institutions belonging to professional associations and at the same time serving the purpose of adult education are the building of the mill owners in Ahmedabad by Le Corbusier and the Sumi Memorial Hall at Ichinomija by Kenzo Tange.

In the United States and Japan as well as in Europe, there are club houses of considerable quality. Here one can compare examples so far removed from each other as the Club House at Mangalia by C. Lazarescu, G. Gheorghiu, C. Ionescu and M. Laurean, and the very attractive, dynamically curved golf club building in Totsuka, erected by Kenzo Tange in 1963, as well as the yacht-club houses on the Danube, such as the one in Budapest by Giorgy Janossi and Zoltan Walko or that in Györ by Janos Lang, both built in 1961. The recreation center of the National Trade Union Council at Hajduszoboszlo, erected by Dezsö Dul in 1963, is a complex consisting of a hotel, a roofed swimming pool and an open-air pool which blend well together in their color scheme.

HOSPITALS

As a result of the achievements of modern medicine the construction of hospitals today represents an unusually complicated task as this requires a multiplicity of inter-related arrangements of rooms, functions and technical installations, to which the architect can only do justice if he possesses an expert knowledge of the needs involved. Thus modern hospitals are for the most part composed of several wings.

Alvar Aalto, with his hospital at Paimio built decades ago, created a prototype for this architectural task. In Japan, Mamoru Yamada in his various hospital constructions decided on a complex consisting of three wings. This basic scheme is also shown by the Czech architect B. Rachmal in his design for the hospital in Brno, and was used in a slightly modified form in the construction of the Mouaser Hospital in Amman, Jordan, by the Italian Marcello d'Olivo. The German hospitals by Werner Hebebrand in Marl and by Harald Deilmann in Bad Salzuflen and in Engelskirchen also proceed from this basic form which is recognized as being particularly practical.

Other large central hospitals of this type were built in Rabat by the architects Delaporte, Bonnemaison and Robert, as well as in Kurle Bu, Ghana, by William Vetter and Kenneth Scott.

In the construction of smaller hospitals or of specialized clinics the spatial arrangement is a less rigid one, as is shown, for example, in the neurological clinic of Narimasu built by Kiyonori Kikutake in 1959, or in Jean François Zevaco's small hospital at Ben Siimane in Morocco.

In the field of modern sanatoriums mention ought to be made of the Sanatorium for Joint and Bone Tuberculosis in Mangalia by Lazarescu and Petrea and of the Health Bath there, built by C. Lazarescu, G.Gheorghiu and N. Laurean.

A new idea is the project for a "Solarium," worked out in 1962 by Vladimir Rubinow, an edifice for the prophylactic use of ultra-violet ray treatment. Here, in cooperation with medical experts, a new-style construction for health treatment purposes has been developed, which, besides containing a large ray treatment hall for 1,300 people, also comprises a lecture hall, a restaurant, rest balconies, changing rooms, bathing pools and consulting rooms.

EDUCATIONAL BUILDINGS

In many countries of the world modern architecture has concentrated on the creation of certain integrated building complexes. Frequently these are concerned with the purposes of higher education. Especially in Latin America, the U.S.A. and Africa, entire university cities were built, and these were intended as symbols of architectural renewal. Venezuela, Mexico, Ghana and various other countries may serve as examples of this. The universities have been given the status of spiritual centers of the countries.

Leading examples of comprehensive campus schemes are the Illinois Institute of Technology by Ludwig Mies van der Rohe, and the buildings for the "Ciudades Universitarias" of Mexico City and Caracas. Other integrated building complexes serving higher education came into being in Rio de Janeiro, Panama, Kumasi, Ibadan

and in Finland, where Alvar Aalto built the technical college in Otaniemi.

During recent years American and Japanese universities have undergone a rapid development. Worthy of special mention are buildings erected for Harvard University – above all the Fine Arts Center by Le Corbusier – the Arts & Communications Center in Andover by Walter Gropius, and the research building of the University of Pennsylvania in Philadelphia by Louis I. Kahn, the School of Art and Architecture of Yale University in New Haven by Paul Rudolph, buildings by J. M. Pei for Honolulu University, as well as the various university buildings in Chicago by Eero Saarinen.

In Japan numerous individual buildings were erected for old universities, as for example the great hall of Gakushuin University by Kunio Mayekawa, the buildings by Hiroshi Oe for the Hosai University, by Antonin Raymond for the Nanzan University in Nagoya and the magnificent Toyoda Auditorium of Nagoya University by Fumihiko Maki. In Cuba the laboratory building of the College of Engineering at Santo Tomas de Villanueva by the architects Manuel R. Gutierrez and Mario G. Suarez may be mentioned.

Of the more recent Eastern European constructions, the Experimental and Research Institute of Medicine in Budapest built by Erwin Kemper in 1961/64 and the Research Institute for Macromolecular Chemistry in Prague by Karel Prager are noteworthy. Important buildings for agricultural schools within the framework of local universities were created in San Salvador by Karl Katstaller and Ehrentraut Schott and at Fujen University near Taipeh on Formosa.

The Polish architect Marek Leykam in 1962/3 designed an Institute of Medicine for the Academy of Sciences in Warsaw. He created an arrangement composed of a multi-storied, round, skyscraper building, a long, flat horizontal tract lit from above, and a large round auditorium. Comparable to this is the post-graduate building of the new Agricultural College in Nitra Czechoslovakia, by Chovanek, which in its turn derives from similar buildings in Latin America, Italy and Japan. In India Doshi erected the Institute of Indology in Ahmedabad, a simple construction made of concrete.

English college buildings are firmly tied to national tradition, and new departures only occur in buildings by Howell, Killick, Partridge and Amis, such as that for St. Ann's College or the project for St. Anthony's College, both in Oxford. Arne Jacobsen designed the new buildings for St. Catherine's College, also in Oxford. Further outstanding educational buildings in England are the work of Frederick Gibberd, James Stirling and James Gowan. In Germany new university buildings came into being in Ulm, Darmstadt, Freiburg, Braunschweig and Bochum.

A fascinating building of the new dynamic style involving the use of the powerful effective qualities of rough concrete was erected in 1960/65, by the Italian architect Enrique Castiglioni for the Instituto Technici i Professionali in Busto Arsizio. Förderer, Otto and Zwimpfer, in the University of Economic and Social Sciences St. Gallen, Switzerland, created a system of rooms of varying height made of concrete. Here works of sculpture were incorporated into the spatial arrangement as a matter of principle.

An attempt is being made to deal with the new situation in Africa by a few centers of re-education such as those realized by Jean François Zevaco. His "Centre de Ré-éducation" in Tit-Mellil is a highly interesting complex with a large lecture hall raised above the ground by base constructions and concrete supports.

Notable new student dormitories are the Aquinas Hostel of Madrid University City by José M. Garcia Paredes and Rafael de la Hoz, and certain student homes in Bucharest by I. Servan and R. Belea, N. Opreanu and A. Köntza and the civil engineers Mihailescu and Boiangian. The Finnish architect Reima Pietilä, in his student hall for Otaniemi University, found an architectural form combining space and volume in a new way.

While contemporary school construction has reached a particularly high degree of maturity – here one only needs to point out the pioneering countries in this field: Switzerland, Britain and Holland – it is nevertheless true that new conceptions in this so important constructional task have only rarely been realized. Outstanding examples are the Tapiola schoolhouse by Kaija and Heikki Siren, Mayfield School by Powell and Moya, Enrico Castiglioni's school in Busto Arsizio, the Indian schools at Kuha by Uttam C. Jain (1961) and at Ahmedabad by B. V. Doshi, the school at Szásvár in Hungary, and the school in Aesch built by Förderer, Otto and Zwimpfer.

SPORTS BUILDINGS

During recent years the construction of sports buildings has gained an ever-growing importance. How important a position this constructional task occupies at the present time became clear especially during the Tokyo Olympics in 1964. Mass sports created special demands in modern cities. Thus great stadiums and sports arenas exist everywhere.

New vistas in this field were opened up by the sports halls of Pier Luigi Nervi and M. Piacentini, i. e. the Palazzo dello Sport, the Palazzetto dello Sport and the great Stadio Flaminio in Rome. Similar to earlier sports buildings by Pier Luigi Nervi, these buildings characterize certain stages in the development of modern architecture. Other outstanding achievements of architecture as a whole were the Japanese sports halls designed for the 1964 Tokyo Olympic Games by Kenzo Tange, Masachika Murata, Yoshinobu Ashihara and Makoto Masuzawa. The dominant position is held by the halls duly completed in 1964 by Kenzo Tange. The great sports hall has the largest hanging roof built to date and can accommodate 13,246 spectators during swimming events and 16,246 for Judo contests.

The hockey stadium of Yale University at New Haven, completed in 1958 by Eero Saarinen, is outstanding because of its dynamic roof construction. Here, too, the technical and artistic efforts were concentrated on creating the dominating roof form which spans the whole building.

Sports constructions of this sort, whether it is a matter of open-air stadiums, outdoor or indoor swimming pools or other works in this field, have, during recent years, come into existence in every part of the world. Thus the sports installations are among the dominant features of the university cities of Caracas and Mexico City. In Poland a central sports area was created in the Mokotov district of Warsaw by the architects Ihnatowicz, Soltan, Tomaszewski and Wittek.

In Zagreb the architect Turina and the engineer Ehrlich built a stadium with an overall capacity of 18,000 spectators. A grandiose ensemble consisting of a sports stadium and a swimming stadium was constructed by M. vann Molyvann and V. Bodiansky at Phnom-Penh in Cambodia. The stadiums in Sweden built by Jaenecke and Samuelson, such as Nya Ulleri in Göteborg, also belong to that country's most important modern constructions. The Sports Hall in Brno, Czechoslovakia has a roof in the shape of a wing-structure and the Bratislava Sports Palace by Josef Chovanec is similar to the Exhibition Hall in Raleigh, North Carolina, with a hanging roof spanning an elliptical floor plan. The Tennis Hall in Budapest, built in 1960 by Jenö Sznedroi and Istvan Mennihart, is in the shape of a simple cupola shell, making an interior space without supports possible. The Bucharest State Circus is one of the most beautiful and most important buildings in the entire country.

Based on the example of the Exhibition Hall in Raleigh, there now exist in numerous countries halls intended for sporting events, which can, however, be put to other uses. In Japan the halls by Kenzo Tange in Shizuoka, by Miyagawa in Niigata and Junzo Sakakura in Saga are notable in this field. In Europe Roland Rainer built halls in this type in Vienna, Bremen and Ludwigshafen. There are also certain projects which endeavor to create new forms for this construction task. In this connection mention must be made of the designs for the Palazzetto dello Sport in Busto Arsizio by Enrico Castiglioni as well as the various attempts by Frei Otto and the architects inspired by him, which are primarily directed to creating buildings for temporary purposes. A simple roof membrane, held up by various degrees of air pressure can be erected at short notice without special effort and dismantled again quickly. An indoor tennis court has already been built according to this principle, and a skating rink at Villars in Switzerland was given a roof consisting of a membrane of this type. Frei Otto designed a similar model for the roller-skating rink in Dortmund.

The work of Richard Buckminster Fuller also offers ideal possibilities for sports buildings. His geodetic cupolas can be used as sports halls as well as for other purposes. As far back as 1959 Buckminster Fuller designed such a sports hall with a diameter of 198 meters (649.6 feet), thus reaching a span never achieved before.

Notable new swimming pools are in the Tokyo stadium by Masachika Murata, the new indoor baths in Leningrad, the beach buildings in Budapest and Kecel in Hungary and the indoor pool in Mainz by the architects Apel and Beckert.

Particularly in recent years attempts have been made to consolidate various types of sports facilities, a good example being the "Centre Omnisport" in France. Henri Maillard has made similar designs for d'Alencion

and so have the American engineers, Goldsmith and Ferris. A swimming pool, a gymnasium, a skating rink, tennis courts and various other installations are all covered by one gigantic, overall roof construction. This may create possibilities to bring players and spectators closer to each other. The purpose here is not for a few to be active while many others watch, but rather to awake in each individual the urge for participation in sports.

OFFICE- AND COMMERCIAL BUILDINGS

Today's economic and social structure has resulted in the fact that in the modern city it is no longer religious or communal buildings which are the central features, but that their place is taken by great office blocks for business firms and corporations, that is to say, for industry, commerce, banking and insurance. A decisive part in determining the size of the buildings is played by the tenants' need to present an impressive appearance. Thus, for advertising purposes, many buildings are directly linked with the names of the firms- the Pirelli skyscraper in Milan, the Seagram Building and the Lever House in New York, the Mannesmann Building and the Phönix-Rheinrohr House in Düsseldorf, etc. These edifices have often, over and above their proper functions, had an effect on the appearance of the city

as a whole, for they opened up and shaped the vertical zone in a way which had not been possible in the past. The conception of the multi-storied office building has been largely determined by the work of Ludwig Mies van der Rohe and his school, from which originated the Lever House in New York as a prototype. This construction has acted as a model throughout the world. The works of Victor Gruen in Los Angeles and of David Libeskind in São Paolo show the skyscraper growing out of a horizontal ground-floor tract, whereby the vertical and the horizontal are related in a new way.

Victor Gruen and Harry Weese, in the great "Shopping Centers" in the United States, found a highly impressive architectural form for this construction task. Another possibility is shown in the shopping center in Lulea, Northern Sweden, accommodated entirely in a structure of several stories and built by Ralph Erskine.

HOTELS AND RESTAURANTS

In the age of mass tourism particular attention has been directed to hotel building. New regions are continuously being opened up for tourism, and here modern, comfortable hotels are created first. Great hotel chains generally lose themselves in showy luxury, which results in architectural monstrosities. In the type of hotel construction deliberately based on the principle of large-scale production and standardization there exist only isolated attempts to solve this construction problem in a suitable way with the methods of industrialization. This tendency is principally evident in the building of holiday camps and motels.

Arne Jacobsen in 1960 completed the hotel and office skyscraper building belonging to an airline company in Copenhagen. Kenzo Tange, in the addition to The Atami Garden Hotel in Atami, created Japan's most outstanding modern hotel building. Noriaki Kurokawa erected the small Hotel Honjima. In Nigeria the firm of Architects Co-Partnership built the Hotel Bristol in Lagos.

Hotel construction has reached a level of remarkable maturity in Eastern Europe, above all in Hungary and Rumania. On the latter country's Black Sea coast there exist, especially in the Mamaia recreation resort region, magnificent achievements of contemporary hotel building. Worthy of special mention are the Park Hotel by

C. Constantinescu and G. Gheorghiu, the Hotel Perla by M. Laurean and the Pescarus Hotel by V. Ritrea. The hotel area on this coast possesses the advantage of having been planned by a general co-ordinator, C. Lazarescu and the civil engineer N. Laszlo, according to an overall conception.

In Hungary, on Lake Balaton, co-ordinated planning is in evidence, but here, also, individual hotels stand out through their excellence, as for example, the hotels built in 1963 in Tihany by Attila Kuhn, the Arany-Homok Hotel in Kecskemet by Istvan Janaki and built in Salgotarian by Giörgy Janossi in 1964.

The task of building motels, too, has found very successful solutions in two instances on Lake Balaton, that by Lajos Földesy in Siófok, built in 1961, and the one in Tihany built in 1960 by Karoli Polony.

Efforts to explore new paths in the construction of holiday facilities were made years ago by Richard Neutra, as in his holiday hotel at Malibu, California. In more recent years he was followed by the Spanish architects Coderch and Valls from Barcelona, with their Torre Valentina projects. These designs comprise a large number of units with the greatest possible isolation ensured for each. In Greece Aris Constantinidis has built some good motels such as the Xenia-Motel in Kalambaka.

In the field of modern restaurant building mention must be made first of all of the construction at Lisanza on Lake Maggiore by Enrico Castiglioni, completed in 1958. Other good restaurants were built in Efori, Rumania, such as the Perla Marii Restaurant by Lazarescu and Popovici, which, like other buildings by these architects, is, in part, directly modelled on Brazilian examples. In Prague the restaurant built for the Brussels World Fair of 1958 by Cubr, Hruby and Pokorny was re-erected on a very beautiful site under the name of "Restaurant Praha." On Lake Balaton, in Hungary, there are also a number of good restaurant buildings such as the Tática in Badascony by Ferenc Callmayer built in 1960. The Swiss architects Förderer and Zwimpfer erected a restaurant at Neuhausen, a concrete construction arranged in many layers. A very interesting solution was found by the Portuguese Siza Vieira in his restaurant situated directly on the coast at Boa Nova. This construction was integrated in a wild, rocky landscape close to the shore.

EXHIBITION BUILDINGS

Halls of various dimensions for permanent or temporary exhibition purposes offer good opportunities for the use of shells or cupolas, as well as other light-weight constructions.

Most of the large exhibition halls are permanent buildings used for annually recurring exhibitions. To this category belong the hall in Turin by Pier Luigi Nervi and the halls for the Tokyo International Trade Center by Masachika Murata. Comparable to the above are the Pavilion of the National Economic Exhibition in Bucharest and the Pavilion Z for the Brno Fair.

Most of the buildings for the World Fairs in Brussels, 1958, and in New York, 1964, and those of the "Expo 64" in Lausanne, on the other hand, were torn down again although they did include important works of modern architecture. Thus, Le Corbusier created the pavilion for the firm of Phillips at Brussels, Reime Pietilä the Finnish Pavilion, and Boucher, Blandel and Filippone, together with the civil engineer Sarger, the Marie Tumas restaurant pavilion. Frei Otto erected various tent constructions for the Federal Garden Shows in Germany. Their flexibility, easy transport and economy make such constructions ideal for modern exhibition purposes. The French Pavilion at the 1958 Brussels World Fair, built by Guilleaume Gillet and René Sarger, was also based on the principle of light-weight construction, so that it was possible to roof-in a large space by the simplest means. The Information Pavilion erected by Sarger in conjunction with Boucher, Blandel and Filippone in the Place de Brouckère in Brussels remained as a permanent installation after the end of the World Fair.

A completely different principle – that of combining very small rod-shaped units – was the basis for the construction of the German Pavilion for the Industrial Exhibition at Khartoum in the Sudan, by G. Lippsmeier and F. Reiser. A Polish design for the Brussels World Fair was based on the same principle, which was also applied for the pavilion created by Theo Crosby for the International Architecture Congress in London.

However, the most decisive contribution to this subject was made by the American Richard Buckminster Fuller, whose geodetic domes have been used in many of the world's cities for temporary exhibitions. Fuller's principle provides an important basic pattern for the work of other architects also. Thus, the "Climatron" by Murphy and Mackey, built in St. Louis for the Botanical Gardens of the state of Missouri convincingly demonstrates the application of Fuller's principles.

Architecturally significant market hall buildings were created by Eduardo Torroja in Spain, by Felix Candela in Mexico, by Mauri in Algeria, by Gori and Ricci in Pescia, by Simon and Morisseau, together with Sarger in Royan, by Cardini in Florence and by Hermkes in Hamburg.

INDUSTRIAL BUILDINGS

A few decades ago industrial building played a decisive part in shaping architectural development. Works by Behrens, Poelzig, Mendelsohn and Gropius gave this constructional task a leading place. In more recent years far-reaching changes took place as a result of alterations in productive processes, and industrial construction lost its prominent position. The variability necessary in this type of construction cannot, in the majority of cases, be reconciled with the use of building materials which are designed to provide durability and are intended for formal methods of construction. Industrial building in its present form is, by nature, a thankless task. The processes of production are changing so rapidly that the architect's work often lags a long way behind.

There are, however, a few industrial buildings which, while they remain bound to tradition, have attracted wide-spread notice and are also of significance for the situation of architecture in general. Notable in this connection among post-war buildings are various installations for General Motors in Detroit by Eero Saarinen, some for Olivetti in Ivrea, others for the handkerchief-weaving establishment in Blumberg by Egon Eiermann, as well as for factories in Braunschweig, Germany and in the Ruhr by Friedrich Wilhelm Krämer and mine buildings and mine-shaft installations in the Ruhr by Fritz Schupp.

Noteworthy industrial buildings in Spain are the work of Ortiz Echague and Raffael Echaide in Barcelona and of Martorell and Oriol Bohigas in Badalona. Harry Weese erected the Dynamometer Testing Building for the Cummins Engine Company in Columbus, Indiana; Bernhard Hermkes, the power station in Wedel near Hamburg. Special mention should also be made of the Danish industrial constructions by Arne Jacobsen. Good solutions were also found in the case of a number of Hungarian installations such as the Telecommunications Technology Factory in Budapest by Lajos Arnoth and Jenö Szendroi, built between 1961 and 1963, the Grape Processing Works and Hothouse in Szekszard by Ferenc Callmayer from the years 1960–62, the Seed Extraction Plant in Dombovar by Attila Emödy, also from the years 1961–63, as well as the chemical combine on the Thai by Laszlo Bajnay, 1960–64. In Bucharest, I. Ionescu built the Mineral Tanning Factory and Costinescu the Unirea Oil Factory in Iasi.

Special architectural features are noticeable in printing plants. G. Leclaire erected the large printing plant in Massy, designed in 1953 and built between 1954 and 1957, Bengt Blasberg and Henrik Jais-Nielsen completed the printing plant in Helsingborg in 1959. The printing plant in Numazu by Kenzo Tange was built as far back as 1953–54.

More modern forms of industrial building were found in the construction of works such as the asbestos cement factory in Lojo, Finland, by Kurt Simberg, which was completed in 1958, the factory halls in Blomberg by Schulze-Fielitz, von Rudloff and von Altenstadt, the buildings for the Butchers' Co-operative in Heidelberg by Lothar Götz and Gerhard Hauss, and the factory built in 1964 for the Nitto-Shokuhin Co. by Noriaki Kurokawa. Marcel Breuer erected a factory in Torrington, Canada, and the "Atelier 5," a group of young Swiss architects, created the building for the boiler factory W. and T. Müller in Thun, Switzerland, built from sifted concrete, which, in addition to the factory installations, contains a level area with a residential building.

Completely new forms for factory building have emerged only in rare cases; notable among these exceptions are the shops built for the firm of Bacardi in Cuantitlan, Mexico, by Felix Candela or the great repair shop of the Union Car Tank Company in Baton Rouge, Louisiana, which was given a gigantic roof construction based on the system of Richard Buckminster Fuller.

When dealing with new tasks in this field as, for example, atomic power stations, one is forced to develop new architectural forms. Among the earliest buildings of this type special mention should be made of the atomic power station at Hinkley Point designed by Frederick Gibberd, the power station of the Munich College of Technology in Garching by Gerhard Weber (1958), the research center of Industrial Reactor Laboratories Inc. in Plainsboro, New Jersey, built in 1958 by Skidmore. Owings and Merrill, the building of the CERN research laboratory in Geneva by Rudolf Steiger

and the atomic reactor in Rehovot, Israel, by Philip Johnson.

In the field of transport buildings such as railway stations, airport buildings, filling stations and airplane hangars, a few spectacular achievments have attracted attention to themselves to this construction task in general. An early example was the Statione Termini building in Rome by Calini and Montuori, while a more recent one is the TWA building at Kennedy airport in New York by Eero Saarinen. Since the construction of Orly and Orbetello there had not been any outstanding solutions in this field. Other airport buildings came into being in Paris/Orly, Copenhagen, Frankfurt-am-Main, Tokyo, London and various United States airports.

Road architecture, too, is gaining more and more in importance. In Los Angeles and San Francisco, speedways have now been merged to form four- and five-story traffic levels. The street as an architectural work has become a complementary attraction to housing construction's linear forms, being arranged in continuous patterns. Both of these spheres, together with other urban installation, must grow closer together to form a new synthesis.

HOME BUILDING

The complex problem of dwelling accommodation in our time must be discussed anew in every country. Here it is a matter of defining the relationship between the individual and the community. The architect's task is to find an expression for this relationship. The various prototypes such as Le Corbusier's Unités d'Habitations, the Brazilian housing projects, built by Affonso Eduardo Reidy and the great complexes of low-cost housing in Caracas by Carlos Raul Villanueva must be reexamined to test their usefulness for present-day conditions of living. It is essential for housing construction for the masses to become industrialized. This has been done most purposefully so far in the Soviet Union and a number of other Eastern European countries.

In the framework of the newly set tasks the exact architectural form of these mass-dwelling houses has become of secondary importance. What is essential are

economy, a rapid pace of construction, the appropriate dimensions of space and above all, the integration into an overall town planning scheme of the dwelling units, which must be linked with recreational and rapid transport facilities.

The importance of the single-family house has diminished in the face of these essential tasks. While there still exist outstanding individual solutions along these lines, they occupy only a subordinate place in the total volume of construction. Only groups of one-family houses combined together in a project will in future retain any justification for their existence. Thus, dealing with the isolated individual family will be less important as a subject for architecture in the coming years than the problem of linking together a large number of family units in a well-functioning community while ensuring complete individual privacy.

However, in many cases, especially in North America and Europe, the construction of single-family houses still provides the experimental ground for the architect wishing to test new materials and forms. Consequently there exist in this field outstanding architectural achievements, but this constructional task in general is limited to catering to small sections of the population. As a model for this genre one may mention the Farnsworth house in Plano, Illinois, by Mies van der Rohe, built in 1955, a private family-dwelling of choice proportions. On a platform raised from the ground by a system of supports there is a living area made of glass, which can be completely curtained off, as well as various open terraces. This type of house has been emulated in many European and Latin American countries, as for instance in the works of the architects David Libeskind, Manuel Rosen, Reginald Caywood Knight, Kenneth Scott, Erik Cristian Sørensen and Jørn Utzon. The single-family dwellings built by the architects Elie Azagury, Affonso Eduardo Reidy, Emery and Miquel, Christian Norberg Schulz, Kiyonori Kikutake, Julian Elliot, Amancio d'Alpoim Quedes, and by the "Atelier 5" group, on the other hand, are indebted to the style of Le Corbusier.

Other types of houses have been developed from shell or circular forms or in the shape of sea shells. In this category belong works by John Mac L. Johansen, Eduardo Catalano, Eliot Noyes, Marcello d'Olivo, Martorell, Oriol Bohigas and Arne Jacobsen.

For future development the possibilities of prefabricated methods of building should prove to be of the greatest importance. Large firms are already supplying serviceable houses to be assembled on the site. Thus there exist prefabricated houses by the French architects Jean Prouvé and Ionel Schein, the American Richard Buckminster Fuller, the Englishman Arthur Quarmby, the Italian Roberto Menghi, the Belgian Renaat Braem, the Austrian Roland Rainer and the German Dieter Schmid. Other American designs are by George Nelson, Charles Eames and by Hamilton and Goody.

THE BUILDING OF HOUSING PROJECTS

Of greater importance than the styles of isolated one-family houses, however excellent these may be, is the grouping and arrangement of several individual houses to form a coherent whole. Housing projects can be arranged in various ways: on flat, level areas, in terraces, in groups of cottages or in a vertical, upward-striving arrangement. Various types of projects will play a decisive role in the future development of architecture. In recent years a large number of terrace projects have been built. In this field remarkable results can be achieved by means of careful arrangement, displacement of units and by utilizing the possibilities of plastic effects.

Kaija and Keikki Siren built projects of this type in Finland; Badani and Roux Dorlut in France; Ralph Erskine, Jaenecke and Samuelson in Sweden. Luigi Cosenza erected settlements in Pozzuoli for Olivetti.

An outstanding individual case is the Halen project near Berne in Switzerland built by the architects' group "Atelier 5," who combined a number of individual private dwellings into a complex which also includes a swimming pool, a garage, a shopping center, as well as other communal institutions. The theme of a terraced residential construction, touched upon in this project, will be of great importance for the future. A convincing achievement of this kind is the settlement at Djennan el Hassan by Roland Simounet. Pure terrace-type housing settlements also came into being in Zug and in Belp, Switzerland, built by the architects Stucky and Meuli. Further projects of this kind were designed by the German architects Roland Frey, Hermann Schröder and Claus Schmidt for the towns of Stuttgart and Marl under the title "residential hills." In 1962 the Israeli architect Leopold Gerstel designed a terraced residential construction for Haifa which follows the ancient Jewish architectural tradition and which he therefore called the "new Ziggurat." The same conception was also the basis for the Yugoslav architect V. Richter's new designs for terraced houses.

In Morocco André Studer combined a group of houses and interior courtyards in a new way in the "Habitat Maroccaine en Pyramide" in 1954. In the settlement near Kristiansborg Castle in Accra the architect Barrett grouped the houses in accordance with the African "compound" idea in such a way that they form a communal area enclosed like a courtyard. Julian Elliot and Philippe Charbonnier, on the basis of this unifying principle, created one of the most beautiful modern residential settlements in Africa, at Elizabethville.

The last-mentioned types of housing projects represent, primarily, results achieved in areas with a low density of population, and it is clear that different forms of mass residential building are required in large towns and certain areas of dense concentration. These include blocks of apartments and multi-storied buildings. A combination of both these possibilities is represented by the great mass residential blocks in South America or in the still more novel forms of the "house city," which, however, have scarcely been realized as yet.

Up to the present the "Unité d'Habitation" type of construction has not yet been replaced by more modern conceptions of any importance. An excellent solution was found by the young Yugoslav architects Zeljko Solar and Bogdan Budimirov in a housing project in Zagreb. According to the "Ju 61" system they created an architectural form made of prefabricated aluminum parts. This industrialized building method is a solution in the spirit of the Machine Age and corresponds to our present social reality. The system is not bound to any particular material, but allows for a great number of variants according to the given conditions.

Housing projects of a traditional type are represented by the houses near the Bucharest North Railroad Station by Bercovichi, Bergizeanu, Alifanti and Elian, by residential projects in Selenograd, Moscow, and in Prague and Brno in Czechoslovakia, as well as by other projects in the United States designed by Mies van der Rohe, Harry Weese and Yan Chun Wong. Outstanding examples of terrace projects linked with communal institutions were created by Affonso Eduardo Reidy in his Pedregulho and Gavea districts in Rio de Janeiro. The Finnish architect Reima Pietilä also designed projects of this type.

Even greater concentrations have been achieved in the housing projects in Caracas by Carlos Raul Villanueva, the Harumi Apartments in Tokyo by Kunio Mayekawa, mass apartment blocks in Hong Kong by Eric Cumine, Palmer and Turner, the Ramat Hadar Apartments in Haifa by M. Mansfeld, the Marina City multi-story apartment blocks in Chicago by Bertrand Goldberg, the Leimatt skyscraper blocks, built on a triangular ground plan at Oberwil in the Canton of Zug by Stucky and Meuli, the residential skyscraper in the Neue Vahr in Bremen by Alvar Aalto, Hungarian and Czech skyscrapers and residential blocks in London by Tecton, Powell and Moya.

THE BUILDING OF CITIES

In spite of the fact that the task of city construction has today assumed a position of central importance, there have been few successful solutions. In city building the aim must be to provide a basis of existence for contemporary society, where the traditions of the past can be continued, while present-day requirements are catered to. The inexorable nature of present-day reality has led to pessimistic pronouncements such as this by Frei Otto: "We need buildings with a human atmosphere. But never before, especially in residential building, has there been so much rigid, immutable construction. Residential quarters are coming into being where nothing – not one window or wall – is variable. We are building petrified houses and are squeezing human beings into them. Man, who today has at his command technical means which only forty years ago could hardly be imagined, can't even manage to create for himself a shelter adaptable to his requirements. He attempts to fit himself into predetermined forms of accommodation, which he has previously put there for himself."

The shaping of entire towns has only been achieved in a few isolated cases. Le Corbusier, Maxwell Fry and Jane Drew created Chandigarh, Lúcio Costa and Oscar Niemeyer Brasília; Constantinos A. Doxiadis is working on the building of Islamabad and in Finland a few minor communities and regions have been reshaped. Towns intended to be focal points of contemporary life have been created in these places, but mainly under conditions which do not fully correspond to present-day requirements.

Ways of escape from the catastrophic chaos of our urban environment are being sought in a series of projects and visions. Kenzo Tange in his project for the extension and completion of the great city of Tokyo, has planned, in the first instance, for a new settlement in Tokyo Bay. This plan, in its traffic arrangement and in its opening up of new building land and of the vertical dimension, represents a new conception of city construction. The importance of this plan can be assessed merely on the basis of the influence it has already exerted on the many forms of residential terraces. Konrad Wachsmann worked out a plan to reshape the appearance of the port area of Genoa. The various means of transportation carriers – airplanes, cars, ships and railways – are to be concentrated at one point and accentuated by a tall administrative building. Wachsmann, too, uses the water as building ground and for the development of new town-planning arrangements.

Yona Friedman, a Hungarian living in Paris, designed projects for building bridges which could be realized in various parts of the world, but especially in the densely populated areas of the old metropolitan cities. His now-famous plan for Paris suggests the creation of elements of city architecture which could be added successively to the built-up areas already in existence.

In recent years new suggestions for city living have multiplied. In Japan it is especially the "Metabolism" group which has been considering the problem of mass residential areas. Highly interesting projects have been created by Kiyonori Kikutake, Noriaki Kurokawa, Fumihiko Maki and Masato Ohtaka, as well as by Akui, Nozawa and Arata Isozaki. Mention should also be made of the visions of the Dutch architect Constant, works by Eckhard Schulze-Fielitz, the "Intra-house" project by Walter Jonas and the publications of the Russian architect B. Borissovski. The construction of the "Habitat 67' terraced projects by Moshe Safdie in Montreal has already begun. Other projects for residential towns were originated by Uzo Nishiyama and by Sven Nyblom. Of outstanding interest are the suggestions for roofing-over Fort Worth, Texas and New York, which could be realized by the system designed by Richard Buckminster Fuller.

Future city building will have to take new dimensions into account. Noboru Kawazoe sees it this way: "The city of the future, whether we like it or not, will have a scale and speed which far surpass human measurements. There will, for example, be mammoth edifices, superblocks and super-speedways. In this environment of superhuman and therefore inhuman lack of restraint in the three power-factors – size, speed and the spirit arising from the first two – something must be found which will bring Man into a relationship with his environment."

Their magnitude and superlative boldness are not the purpose of such conceptions but rather consequences arising out of contemporary requirements. It would be a misconstruction of the facts if one believed that in the great cities of the future there were any justification for isolated private family houses or for rows of buildings of three to five stories. The steady growth of population was, until now, the characteristic property of large cities, and it would be disastrous to close one's eyes to this development. The possibilities of fulfilling Man's present-day requirements in a city like this, which far surpasses human proportions, in such a way that one can speak for the first time of a Humanist architecture, are certainly present. Technical progress has created the necessary pre-conditions for this, and it is Man's task to utilize these according to the actual given circumstances.

CONCLUSION

At the conclusion of this survey the question about the legitimacy of the traditional conception of architecture must once again be raised. Architecture is not the given premise, but rather the aim for which we are striving. The question arises whether the traditional idea still suffices for us, for that which is taught as architecture in schools and seen as such by the public no longer corresponds with our present-day reality.

The new reality, in which we live, created by the advances of technology, and which we have accepted and are utilizing, is characterized by industrial mass production of goods and in communal efforts such as research into the problems of atomic energy or space travel. In these fields, which are considered vital, there exist national programs in which all the efforts, including those made on an international scale, are combined. While in the past an age was primarily characterized by its architecture, one speaks today of the Atomic Age or the Age of Space Travel. Does this contradiction between past and present perhaps express that conflict between emotion and reason which has been the cause of so many insupportable results which today are almost accepted as normal?

Decades ago the classics of modern architecture were already endeavoring to transform the concept to total planning into reality. The aim was to determine the forms of all usable commodities, from the smallest to the largest, in accordance with the universal concepts of a new urbanism, on the technical basis of industrialized production and in harmony with the modern sociological conditions of mass urban living. If one asks which of these aims has actually been realized, one must necessarily arrive at pessimistic conclusions. Today the importance no longer lies in individual buildings, not even when these can be described, from the point of view of traditional architectural criticism, as being of high quality. Modern architecture must be seen on a world scale. The whole of the world is our field of endeavor; it is the concern of everyone what happens in India, China, Africa, South America, in the rural areas, in the suburban areas, in the slums, the shanty towns and the refugee camps.

What are the architects doing towards the solution of these problems? In most cases they simply ignore them. The relation of one building to another, to the environment, to the landscape, is hardly ever taken into consideration. With the training they have received up till now, architects must fail in their task.

The question therefore arises whether under these circumstances it is possible to speak of a "contemporary architecture" at all. Are we still able to make use of the conception of architecture taught in the colleges or handed down to us from past ages, or is it necessary to develop a new conception based on present-day requirements? After all, culture in general or architecture by no means cease to exist when certain traditional forms no longer correspond with the needs of a changed reality.

What then should be the nature of the new conception of contemporary architecture? On which premises should the efforts towards creating it be based?

In the first place it must be broadened, developing towards the principle of overall town planning. To an ever-greater extent emphasis will be on integrated schemes with less and less stress on isolated individual buildings. Even the finest building fails its purpose and has no function if it is not linked with its surroundings. Second, it is important to revise the conception of architecture from the point of view of industrialization. Today one can surely no longer set out to create architecture on a craft basis, which is an outmoded social form. The individual parts, indeed the individual structure of buildings must today be able to be reproduced on a large scale.

Third, more stress must be laid on the quantitative factor, for today it is essential to build homes for vast numbers of people. Therefore it is not the individual house which must occupy a position of central importance but the mass dwelling in every possible form, to house the millions who have remained homeless until today.

Fourth, within the framework of this new definition of architecture variability will have to play an important part. Rigid installations which even at the time of completion no longer fulfill their required function will have to be avoided, and in designing the structure of a building, methods will have to be developed which ensure the possibility of fulfilling varied and changing demands made in the individual areas.

Fifth, this new conception would have to make provisions for the integration of sculpture and painting, based on the principle of the interrelation of the effective spheres of the various arts. Works of painting and sculpture must not be "stuck on" to a piece of architecture, but must be merged into its structure to form an inseparable whole.

Sixth, economy will be of decisive importance in our new conception. Monuments to the greatness of individuals or communities belong to the past. The criterion of the most comprehensive usefulness must take the place of building for prestige.

It must be the general aim to overcome the importance of technology and science as factors determining the nature of architecture. We must see in them means of creating certain definite architectural effects, means to an end, which is to achieve a viable unified conception.

PLATES

Le Corbusier: Parliament building in Chandigarh, India

Oscar Niemeyer: Congress building in Brasília
Square of the Three Powers. Top – night view

Oscar Niemeyer: President's Palace in Brasília

Mies van der Rohe; Schmidt, Garden and Erikson;
C. F. Murphy Associates; A. Epstein and Sons, Inc.: Federal
center in Chicago

C. F. Murphy Associates; Loebl, Schlossmann and Bennett;
Skidmore, Owings and Merrill: Community center in Chicago

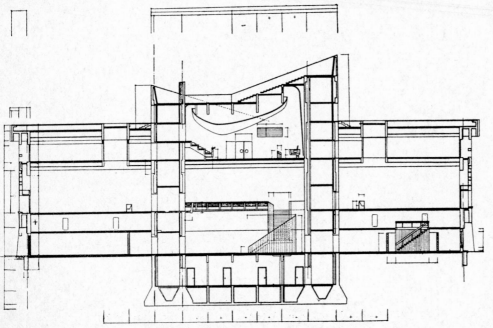

Kenzo Tange: Town Hall in Kuarshiki,
Japan. Left – section

Right – Takeo Sato:
Town all in Iwakuni, Japan
Bottom – K. Lund and N. Slaato:
Community center in Asker, near Oslo

Office Building of Kingi region in the Ministry of Building Construction (design Katayama): Administrative building of the Nara Prefecture, Nara, Japan. Top-aerial view. Bottom-general view

Top – A. Mansfeld and D. Havkin: City Hall in Jerusalem, (model)
Bottom – Y. C. Wong: Competition design for the City Hall in Boston (model)

M. V. Posokhin; A. A. Mdoyantz; E. N. Stamo; P. P. Steller
(architects,) G. N. Lvov; A. N. Kondratiev; S. J. Shkolnikov;
T. A. Melik-Arakelyan (engineers): Palace of Congresses,
Kremlin, Moscow. Right-hall for spectators

Kunio Mayekawa: Festival Hall in Tokyo. Right-detail of main
entrance

Top – Peking Institute of Architecture: Great Hall of the
People in Peking

Bottom – Breuer, Zehrfuss and Nervi: Unesco Building in Paris,
Assembly Hall of the Executive Council

Top – H. Maicu; T. Ricci and I. Serban (architects), A. Cis-migiu; D. Badea (engineers): Palace of the Rumanian People's Republic in Bucharest (Main Hall)
Bottom – Abel and Gutbrod: Liederhalle Concert House in Stuttgart (Beethoven Hall)

Kenzo Tange: Cultural center at Nichinan, Japan
Left-detail of Main Hall

Top – Lagneau and Audigier (architects) and R. Sarger
(engineer): Museum in Le Havre, France
Bottom – Karl Schwanzer: Museum of the Twentieth Century
in Vienna

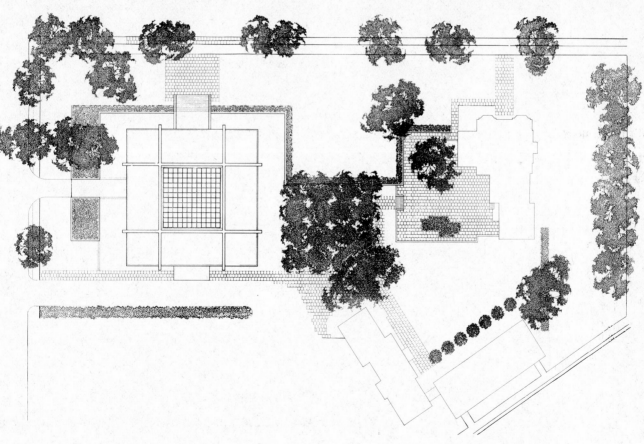

Philip Johnson: Museum in Utica, New York
Bottom – site plan

Ieoh Ming Pei: Museum in Syracuse, New York (project)
Bottom – ground plan

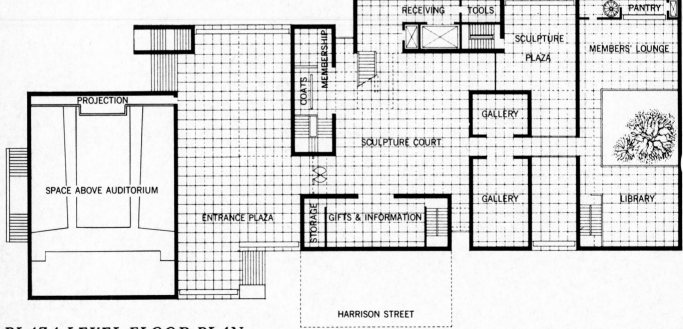

PLAZA LEVEL FLOOR PLAN

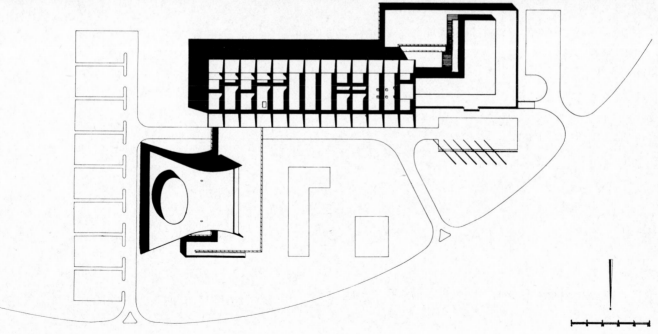

Affonso Eduardo Reidy: Museum of Modern Art in Rio de
Janeiro. Top – inner courtyard
Bottom – site plan

Top – Drake and Lasdun: Museum in Accra, Ghana
Bottom – A. Korabielnikov; S. Kuchanov; A. Kuzmin (architects); J. Avrutin (engineer): Panorama Museum in Moscow

Top – Karl Katstaller and Ehrentraut Schott: State Museum in
San Salvador
Bottom – Philip Johnson: Museum at Fort Worth, Texas

Bassi and Boschetti: Museum of Modern Art in Turin

Al Mansfeld and Dora Gad: Israel Museum in Jerusalem.
Top – general view. Bottom – model

Powell and Moya: Theatre in Chichester, England
Bottom – floor plan and section

Right – Harry Weese: Theatre in Washington, D. C.
Top – exterior view. Bottom – arena stage

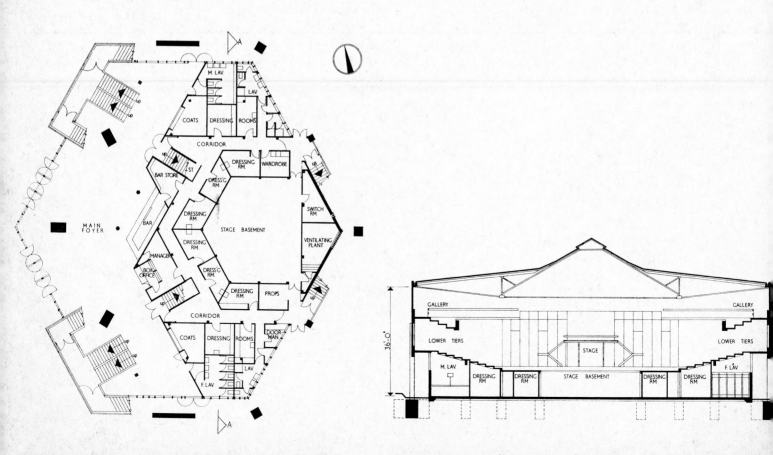

Top – Noriaki Kurokawa: Open-air theatre (model)

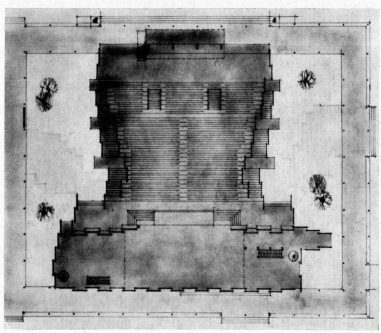

Cezar Lazarescu and I. S. C. A. S.: Summer theatre at Mamaia, Rumania.
Top – detail. Bottom – site plan
Bottom left side – general view

Top – Frei Otto: Open-air theatre in Wunsiedel, Bavaria (model)
Bottom – concert stage in Melbourne, Australia

A. Kotli; S. Sepman; U. Gelnus (architects), E. Paalman
(engineer): Choral stage in Vilno, Lithuanian Soviet Republic.

Peter Molnár: "Köbánya" Cinema in Budapest

Top – G. Mularidis and Y. Goldenberg: Cinema in Bucharest.
Bottom – Josef Kaiser: Kosmos Movie House in Berlin,
Karl-Marx-Allee

Antonin Raymond and L. L. Rado: Concert hall in Takasaki,
Japan. Top – exterior view. Bottom – interior

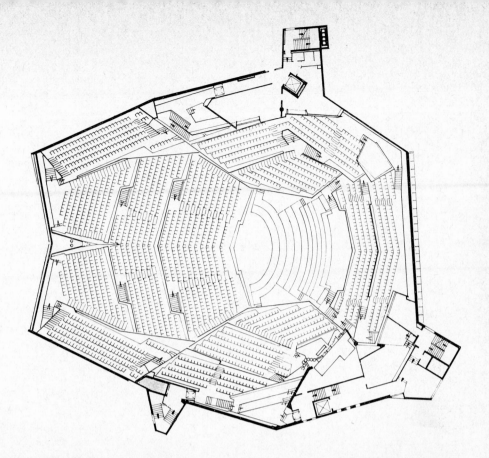

Hans Scharoun: "Philharmonie" in Berlin
Top – floor plan. Bottom – large hall

Viljo Revell: Chapel in Tampere, Finland.
Right – Eero Saarinen: Chapel of Concordia College at Fort
Wayne, Indiana
Bottom – site plan

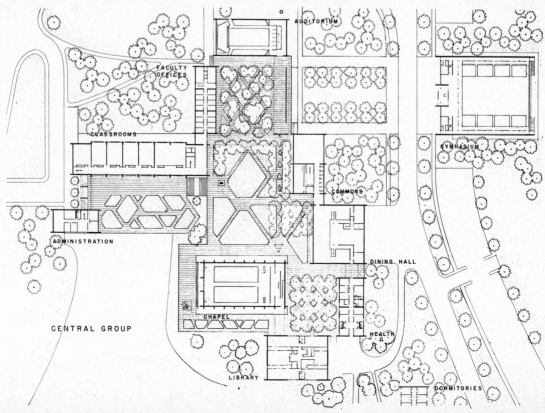

AUDITORIUM

FACULTY
OFFICES

CLASSROOMS

GYMNASIUM

ADMINISTRATION

COMMONS

DINING HALL

CHAPEL

HEALTH

CENTRAL GROUP

LIBRARY

DORMITORIES

Ernst Gisel: Church at Effretikon, Switzerland.

Guillaume Gillet: Church at Royan, France.

Ieoh Ming Pei: Chapel of Tunghai University, near Taichung
Top – night view. Bottom – floor plan
Top right – detail. Bottom right – general view

Felix Candela: Chapel in Coyoacan, Mexico. Top – general
view. Bottom – interior

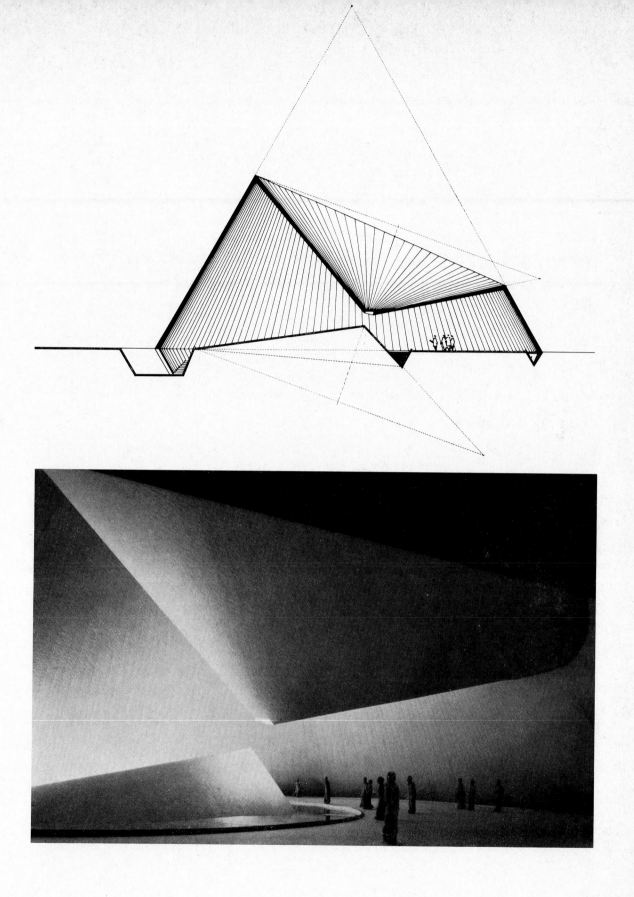

Al Mansfeld: Mausoleum in Rangoon, Burma (model).
Top – section. Bottom – interior

Amancio d'Alpoim Guedes: Kindergarten in Lourenco
Marques, Mozambique.
Top – general view. Bottom – detail

Aldo van Eyck: Children's home in Amsterdam (Municipal Orphanage)

A. T. Polyanski; D. S. Vitukhin; N. E. Gigovskaya (architects),
J. V. Razkevich and J. S. Rabinovich (engineers): Youth camp
Morsko, Artek, Crimea
Top – pavilion. Top right – general view. Bottom – dormitory
tracts

A. T. Polyanski and V. J. Somov: Donbas Rest Home in
Massandra, Crimea. Top – general view. Bottom – dormitory
tracts

Dezsö Dul: Rest home of the National Trade Union Council
at Hajduszoboszlo, Hungary.

Kenzo Tange: Golf Club building in Totsuka, Japan, (interior)
Top left – general view. Bottom – detail of terrace

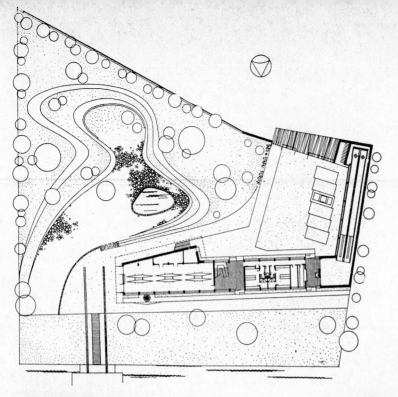

Janos Lang: Boat Club house in Györ, Hungary.
Top – site plan

Noriaki Kurokawa: Children's playground in Tokyo

César Ortiz Echague, Rafael de la Joya Castro and Manuel Barbero Rebolledo: Communal rooms of an automobile factory in Barcelona. Top – interior courtyard. Bottom – dining room. Left – Noriaki Kurokawa: Community center in Kyoto, Japan.

Top – Michael Laird: Children's section of a hospital in
Edinburgh, Scotland.
Bottom – Marcello d'Olivio: Hospital in Amman, Jordan.

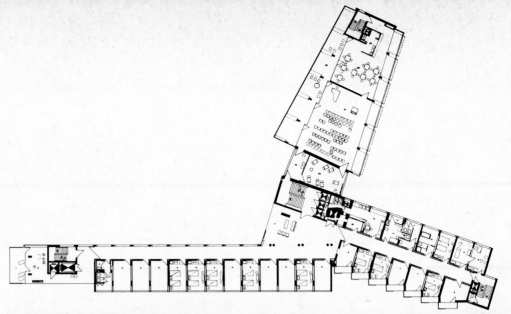

Harald Deilmann: Sanatoria in Bad Salzuflen, Germany.
Top – floor plan (3. floor)

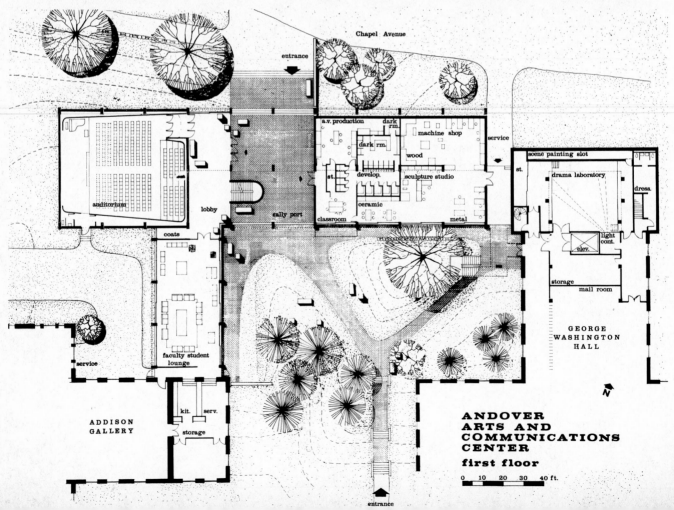

Chapel Avenue

entrance

a.v. production   dark rm.

machine shop

service

dark rm.

wood

st.

scene painting slot

auditorium

lobby

st.

develop.

drama laboratory

dress.

sculpture studio

rally port

ceramic

light cont.

classroom

metal

elev.

coats

storage   mail room

service

GEORGE
WASHINGTON
HALL

faculty student
lounge

service

ADDISON
GALLERY

kit.   serv.

storage

**ANDOVER
ARTS AND
COMMUNICATIONS
CENTER
first floor**

0   10   20   30   40 ft.

entrance

Le Corbusier: Carpenter Fine Arts Center, Harvard University,
Cambridge, Massachusetts
Left – The Architects Collaborative: Art Center of the Phillips
Academy in Andover, Massachusetts.
Bottom – plan

Kunio Mayekawa: Building of the Gakushuin University in
Tokyo
Right – great hall

Top – Post-graduate block of the Agricultural College in Nitra, Czechoslovakia.
Bottom – Building of the Domestic Science Department of Fujen University near Taipei, Formosa.

Top – Karl Katstaller and Ehrentraut Schott: State Agricultural College at San Andres, San Salvador, Festival Hall.
Bottom – B. V. Doshi: Institute of Indology in Ahmedabad, India. From the west

Frederick Gibberd: Institute of Technology in Bath, England.

Top – Carlos Raúl Villanueva: Universidad del Zulia in Mara-
caibo, Venezuela.
Bottom – Antonin Raymond and L. L. Rado: Nanzan University in Nagoya, Japan.

James Stirling and James Gowan: Engineering department
of Leicester University, England. Bottom – floor plan

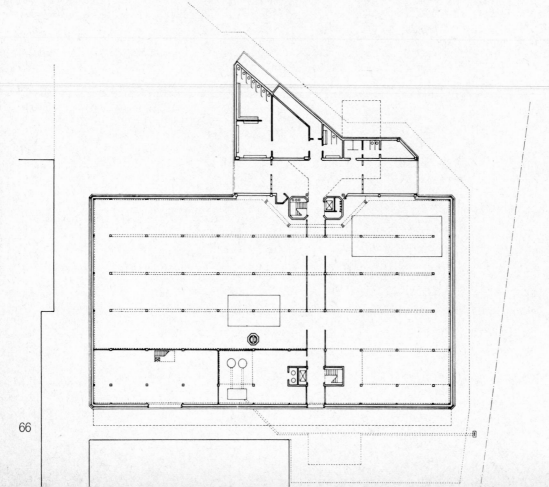

James Stirling and James Gowan: Institute of History at Cambridge University (model). Bottom – section

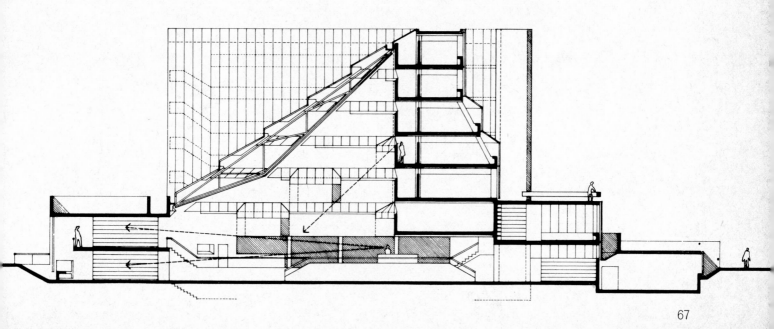

Kunio Mayekawa: Library of Gakushuin University in Tokyo

Kenzo Tange: Library of Rikkyo University in Tokyo. Reading room on first floor

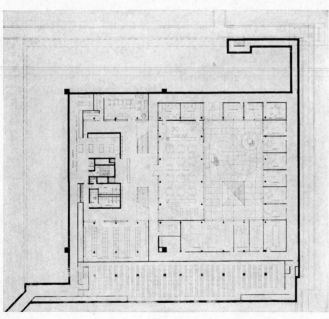

Skidmore, Owings and Merrill: Library of Yale University,
New Haven, Connecticut
Top – reading room. Bottom – floor plan. Right – exterior view

Arne Jacobsen: St. Catherine's College, Oxford.
Top – courtyard. Bottom – refectory

Howell, Killick, Partridge and Amis: St. Anne's College, Oxford. Top – St. Anthony's College in Oxford (model)

Förderer, Otto and Zwimpfer: College of Economic and Social
Sciences in St. Gallen. Switzerland. Top – exterior staircase.
Bottom – cross-section of main building. Right – staircase

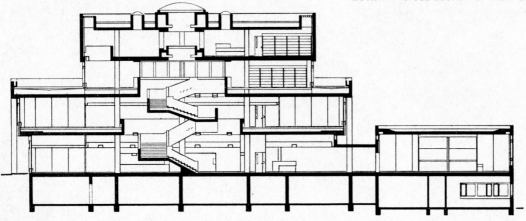

Enrico Castiglioni (architect), Carlo Fontana (engineer):
Vocational school in Busto Arsizio, Italy.

76

Top – Kàroly Surdahelji, Z. Megyeri, M. Hegybirò:
School in Szàszvàr, Hungary.
Bottom – Kaija and Heikki Siren: School in Tapiola, Finland.

B. V. Doshi: School in Ahmedabad, India.

Förderer, Otto and Zwimpfer: Secondary school in Aesch, Switzerland. Top – classroom buildings. Bottom – section and floor plan. Right – hall in classroom building

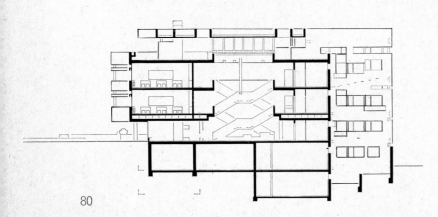

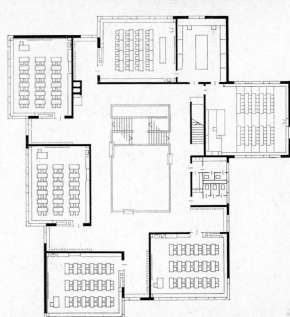

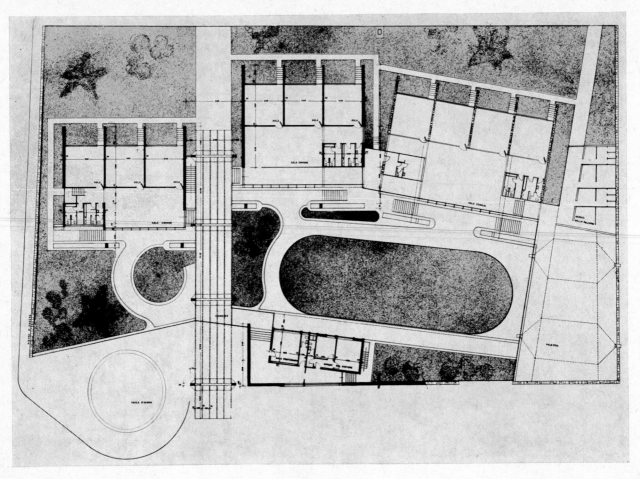

Enrico Castiglioni: School in Busto Arsizio, Italy. Top left –
classroom building. Bottom left – floor plan. Bottom – detail
of outer wall

Pier Luigi Nervi and M. Piacentini: Great sports hall in Rome.
Top – interior. Bottom – exterior view

Top – A. Vitellozzi and Pier Luigi Nervi: Small sports hall in Rome. Below – Vissuzaine-Longuet and Riviere (architects), R. Sarger (engineer): Sports hall at Saint-Nazaire, France (model)

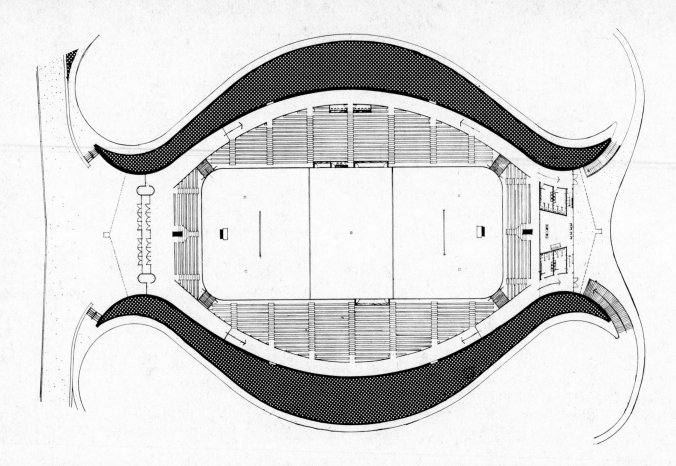

Eero Saarinen: Hockey stadium in New Haven, Connecticut.
Top – floor plan. Below – entrance side. Right – interior

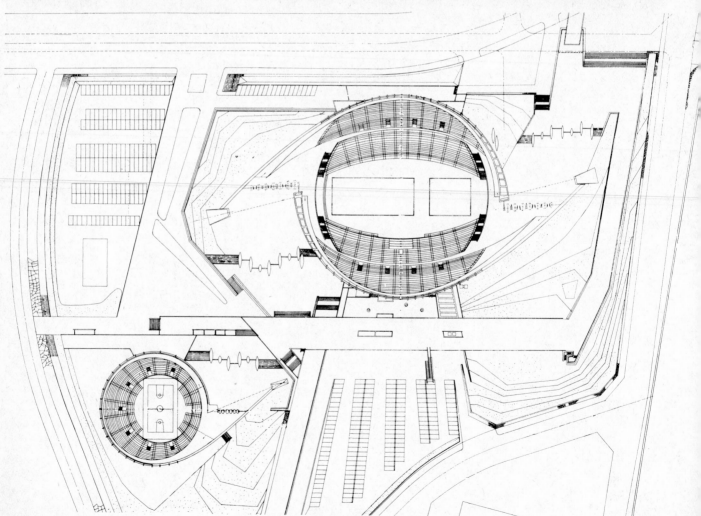

Kenzo Tange: Sports halls in Tokyo. Top – view from south.
Bottom – great hall (section)
Top left – great hall. Bottom left – plan of the entire complex.

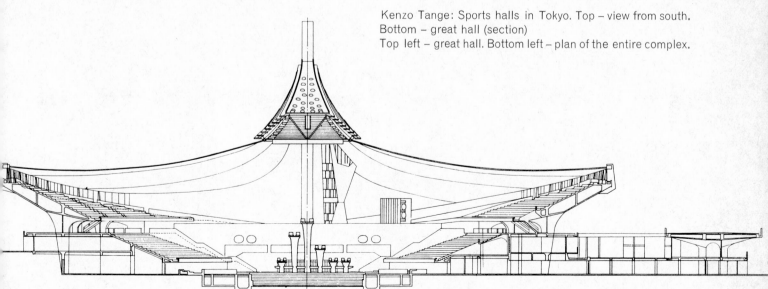

Kenzo Tange: Sports halls in Tokyo. Top – aerial view.
Bottom – interior of great hall. Right – interior of great hall

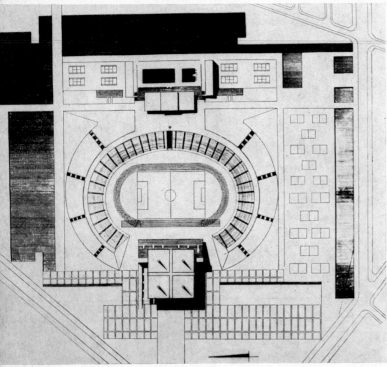

M. vann Molyvann and V. Bodiansky, Mean Kimly, Um Sa-
muth, Gerald H. Hanning, Claude Duchemin, Jean-Claude
Morin and Vladimir Kandaouroff: Stadium in Phnom-Penh,
Cambodia. Top – general view. Bottom – plan

Right – Roland Rainer: Sports Hall in Ludwigshafen, Germany. Top – general view. Bottom – floor plan

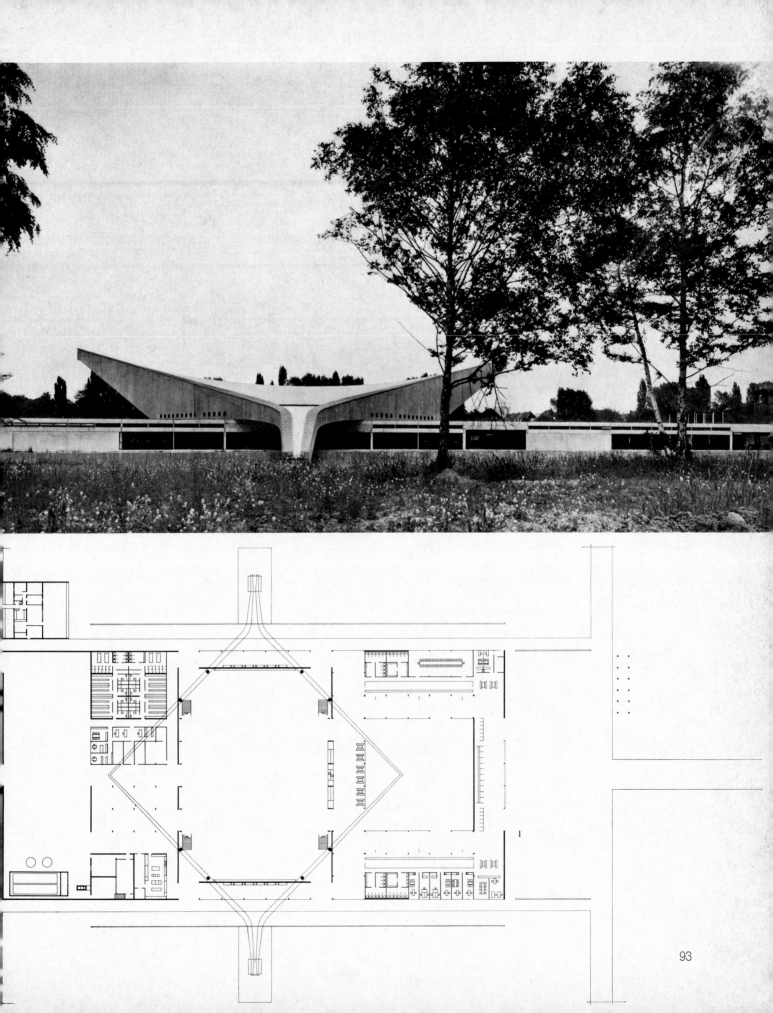

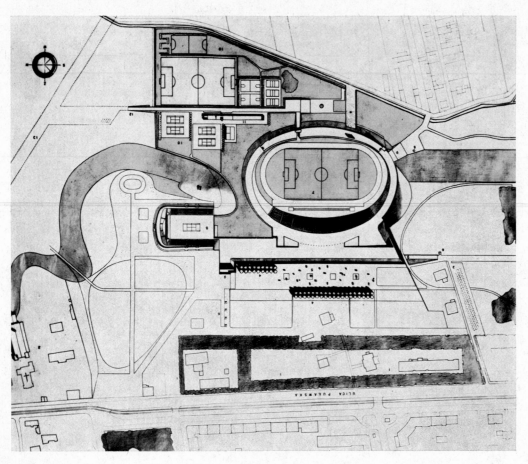

Zbigniew Ihnatowicz, Jerzy Soltan, L. Tomaszewski (architects), W. Wittek, W. Fangor and F. Strynkiewicz (painters and sculptors): Sports center in Warsaw-Mokotow. Entrance

Left – stands and floor plan

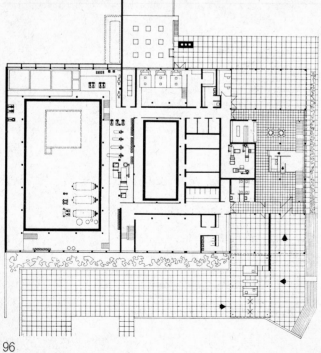

Apel and Beckert: Indoor swimming pool in Mainz, Germany
Top – general view. Middle – swimming pool. Bottom – floor
plan, ground floor

S. J. Yevdokimov and A. P. Ysoitko (architects); L. F. Onyezhsky and V. F. Minin (engineers): Indoor swimming pool in Leningrad

Carlos Raúl Villanueva: Swimming stadium in Caracas.
Top – high diving board and spectators' gallery.
Bottom – general view

Top – Kàroly Jurcsik: Swimming pool in Kecel, Hungary.
Bottom – Làszlo Ivànyi: Shore buildings in Budapest

99

Top – Josef Chovanek: Sports hall in Bratislava, Czechoslovakia.

Bottom – M. Metrich and M. Kopp (architects); R. Sarger (engineer): Sports center in St. Quen, France, (model)

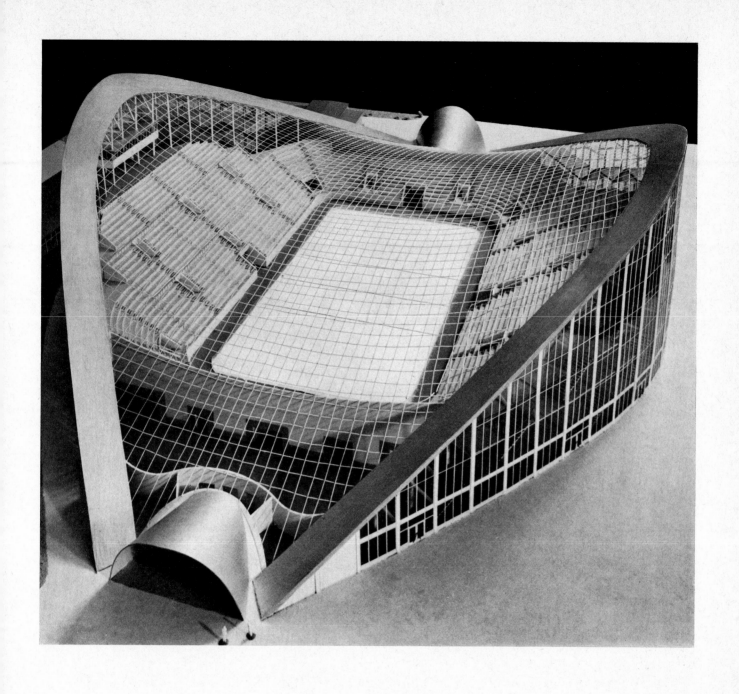

Walter Litzkow and Karl-Heinz Lübke: Skating stadium in Rostock, Germany, (model)

N. Porumbescu, C. Rulea, S. Bercovici, N. Pruncu (architects); A. Lupescu, N. Ardare, V. Vasilache (engineers): State circus in Bucharest. Top left – exterior view, detail. Bottom – interior view

Ludwig Mies van der Rohe: Seagram building in New York

Hentrich and Petschnigg: Phoenix-Rheinrohr skyscraper in
Düsseldorf

Skidmore, Owings and Merrill: Administrative building for
the Business Men's Assurance Co. of America, Kansas City,
Missouri

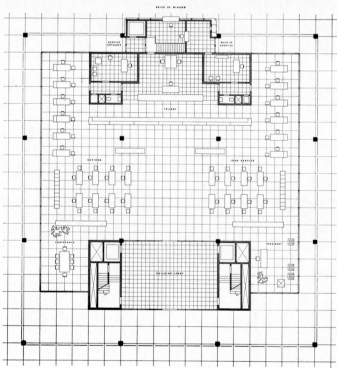

Ludwig Mies van der Rohe: Administrative building of the Home Federal Savings and Loan Association in Des Moines, Iowa.
Bottom – floor plan

Ludwig Mies van der Rohe: Administrative building of the
Bacardi S. A. in Mexico City.

Right – staircase

Ieoh Ming Pei: Skyscraper in Honolulu, Hawaii (model)   Enrico Castiglioni: Skyscraper in Buenos Aires (model)

Kenzo Tange: Skyscraper in Tokyo (model)

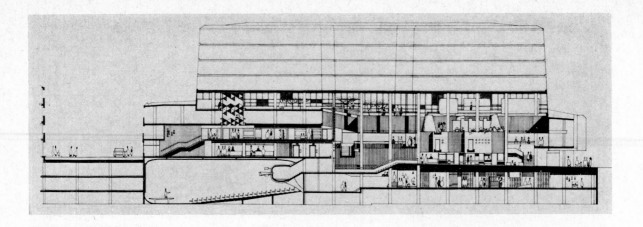

Ralph Erskine: Shopping center in Lulea, Sweden.
Top – section. Bottom – interior

112

Top – Victor Gruen: Eastland Shopping Center in Detroit, Michigan. Bottom – Harry Weese: Hyde Park Shopping Center in Chicago, Illinois

György Jánossy: Hotel Karancs in Salgótarján, Hungary.

Top right – floor plan

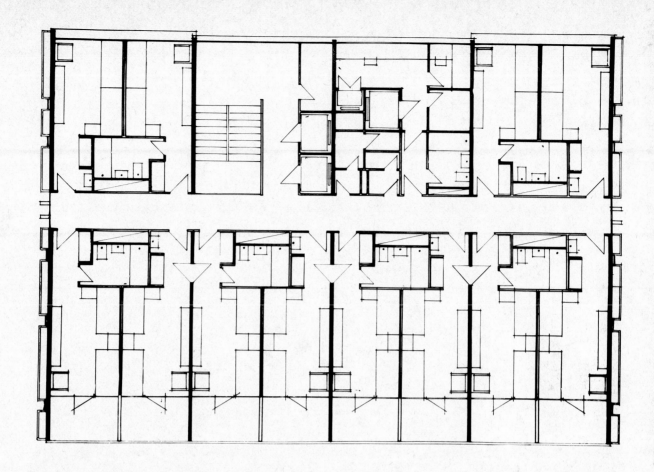

Attila Kun: Hotel in Tihany on Lake Balaton, Hungary.

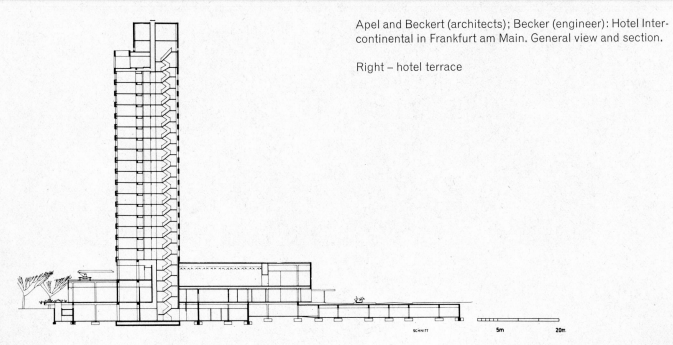

Apel and Beckert (architects); Becker (engineer): Hotel Inter-
continental in Frankfurt am Main. General view and section.

Right – hotel terrace

SCHNITT   5m   20m.

V. Constantinescu and G. Gheorghiu: Park Hotel in Mamaia,
Rumania.

Arne Jacobsen: SAS Building and Royal Hotel in Copenhagen.

Fouroughi, Zafar; Sadegh and Ghiai; Raglan Squire: Hotel in Teheran.

Left – Kenzo Tange: Hotel in Atami, Japan.

Lajos Földesi: Motel at Siófok on Lake Balaton, Hungary.

Right – floor plan

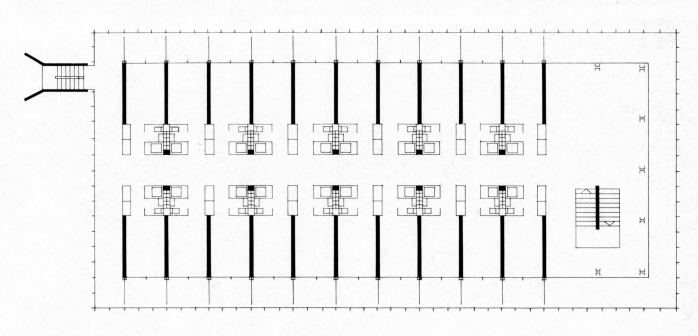

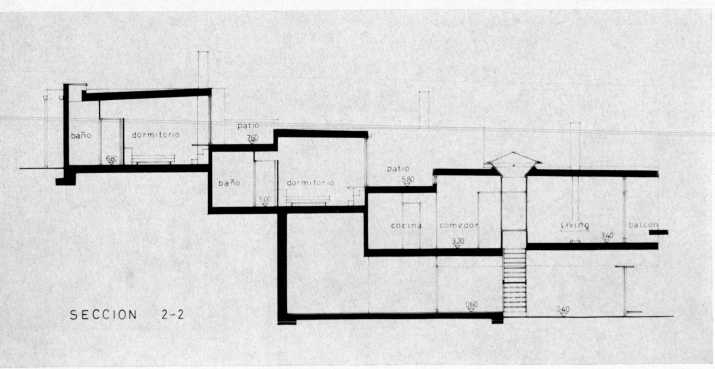

SECCION 2-2

baño dormitorio
patio
baño dormitorio
patio
cocina comedor
living balcon

Coderch and Valls: Holiday hotel Torre Valentina, Spain
(model)
Bottom – section

124

Noriaki Kurokawa: Hotel in Honjima, Japan.

Top – C. Lazarescu, L. Popovichi (architects); N. Laszlo
(engineer): Perla Marii Restaurant in Eforie II, Rumania.

Bottom – Ferenc Callmayer: Tátika Restaurant in Badascony
on Lake Balaton, Hungary.

Top – C. Lazarescu and L. Popovichi: Restaurant in Eforie I, Rumania.

Bottom – Enrico Castiglioni: Restaurant in Lisanza, Italy.

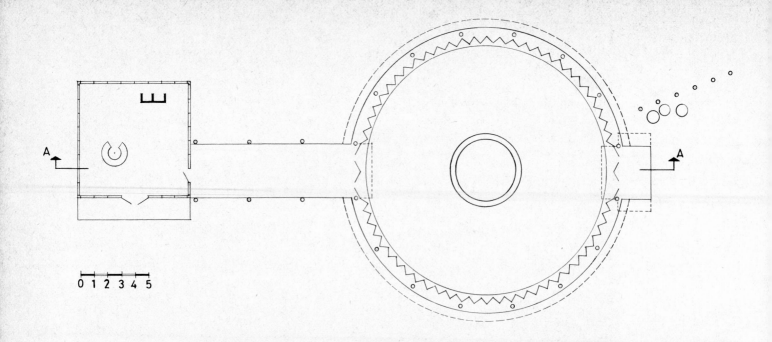

Attila Emödi: Pavilion in Budapest. Top – floor plan
Bottom – interior.

Top right – section.

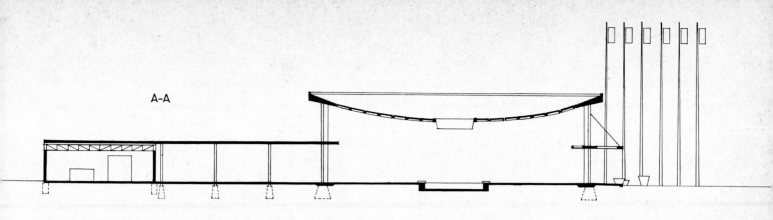

A-A

Pavilion of the agricultural exhibition in Bucharest

Theo Crosby: Pavilion in London.

Top – Pier Luigi Nervi and A. Nervi: Exhibition hall in Turin.
Bottom – Gerardo Clusellas: Pavilion in Mendoza, Argentina.

M. J. Saugey: Exhibition buildings in the 'Expo 64' in Lausanne, Switzerland. Top – 'Port', Bottom – 'Casino'

Frei Otto: Exhibition buildings for the International Garden
Show in Hamburg

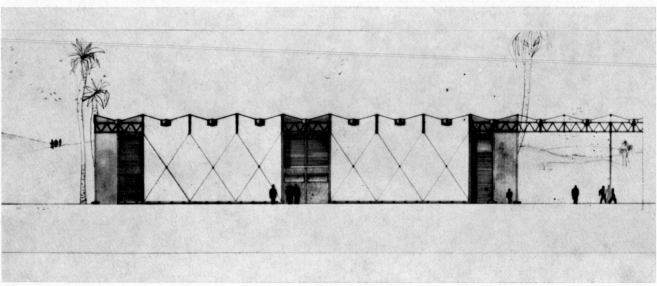

Jerzy Soltan: Polish standard pavilion for industrial fairs in
the tropics.
Top – general view. Bottom – section

Bernhard Hermkes: Plant exhibition buildings in the Botanical
Gardens in Hamburg. Top – general view. Bottom – interior

Richard Buckminster Fuller: Climatron in St. Louis, Missouri.

Left – detail of interior

Marcel Breuer: Factory in Torrington, Canada.

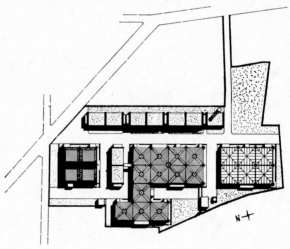

Noriaki Kurokawa: Factory in Sagae, Japan.
Bottom – site plan

Harry Weese: Inspection building of a machine factory in
Columbus, Indiana

140

S. J. Burdo (architect); S. N. Dobrinin, A. S. Shevelev, A. V. Maso, B. V. Barkalov (engineers): Large workshop of a textile factory in Moscow-Noviye Cheremushki

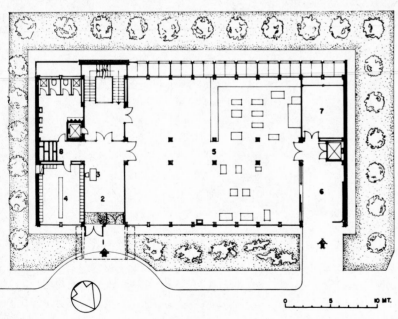

Cesar Ortiz Echague and Rafael Echaide: Automobile factory
in Barcelona.
Bottom – floor plan

Atelier 5: Boiler factory W. & P. Müller in Thun, Switzerland.

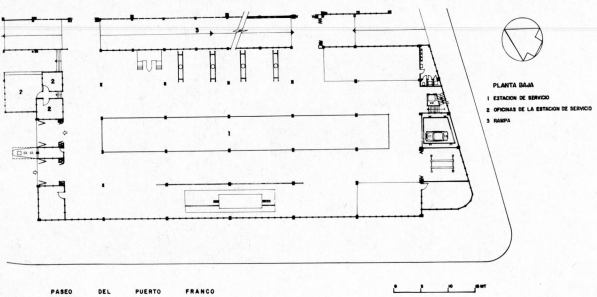

PLANTA BAJA

1 ESTACION DE SERVICIO
2 OFICINAS DE LA ESTACION DE SERVICIO
3 RAMPA

PASEO DEL PUERTO FRANCO

Cesar Ortiz Echague and Rafael Echaide: Factory in Barcelona.
Bottom – floor plan

Lajos Arnoth and Jenö Szendroi: Telecommunications Technology factory in Budapest

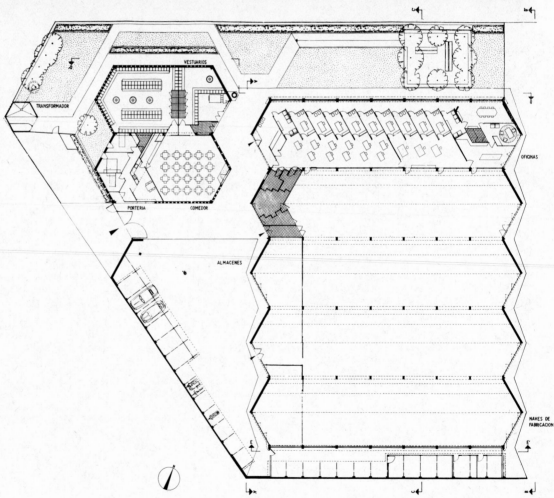

J. M. Martorell and Oriol Bohigas: Factory in Badalona
(Barcelona).
Bottom – floor plan

Bernhard Hermkes: Power station in Wedel, Germany.
Top – general view. Bottom – interior

Top – Laszlo Bajnay: Chemical combine on the River Tisza,
Hungary.
Bottom – Costinescu: Oil factory Unirea in Jasi, Rumania.

148

Top – Arne Jacobsen: Factory in Aalborg, Denmark.
Bottom – Arne Jacobsen: Chocolate factory in Ballerup, Denmark.

Frederick Gibberd: Atomic reactor at Hinkley Point, England.
Top – general view. Bottom – site plan

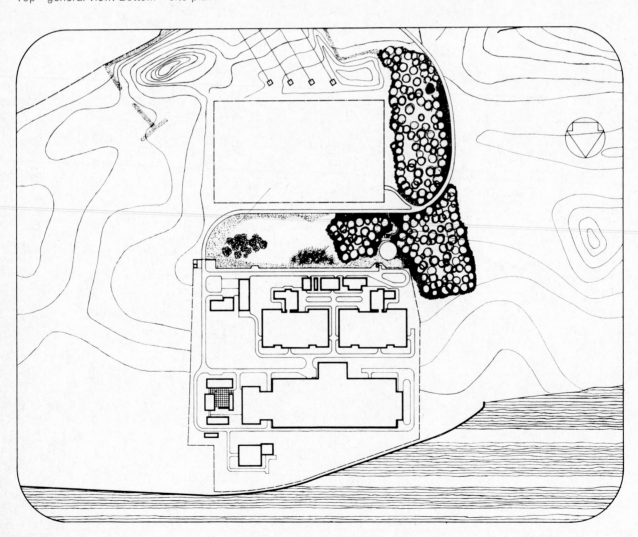

Right – Philip Johnson: Atomic reactor at Rehovot, Israel.
Bottom – floor plan

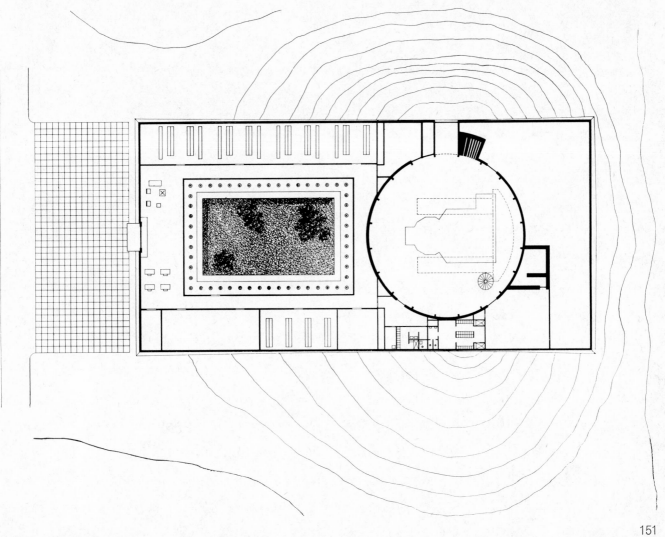

Gerhard Weber: Atomic reactor of Munich Technological
College in Garching, Germany.

Skidmore, Owings and Merrill: Atomic reactor at Plainboro, New Jersey

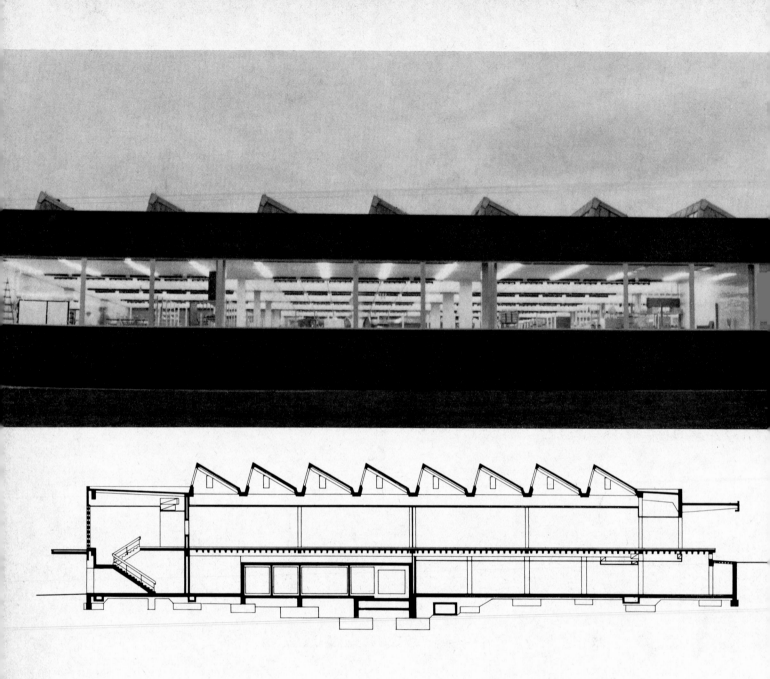

Apel and Beckert: Lufthansa airport service building at Frankfurt am Main. Top – general view. Bottom – section.

Right – Frederick Gibberd: Airport building in London. Top – entrance side. Bottom – hall

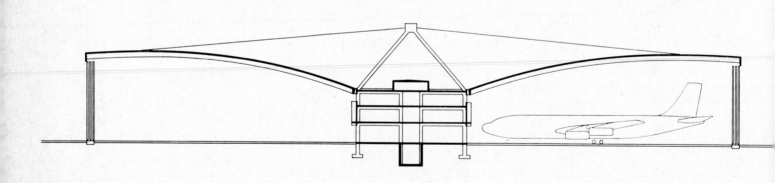

Apel and Beckert: Airport hall in Frankfurt am Main.
Top – general view. Bottom – section

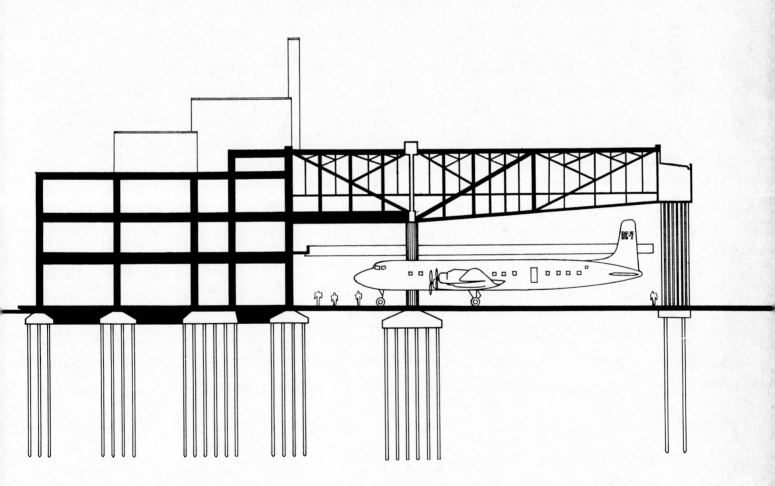

Fuminaga Kiyota: Aircraft hangar in Tokyo. Top – general
view. Bottom – section

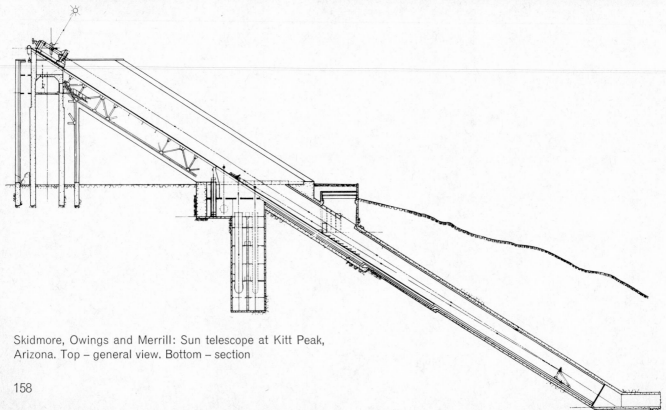

Skidmore, Owings and Merrill: Sun telescope at Kitt Peak,
Arizona. Top – general view. Bottom – section

M. Hofer: Television tower at Miskolc, Hungary.

N. Vasilescu and E. Titaru: Lighthouse at Constanta, Rumania.

Top – José M. Martorell and Oriol Bohigas: Dwelling house in
Cabuls, Spain.

Bottom – Arne Jacobsen: Dwelling house in Odden, Denmark.

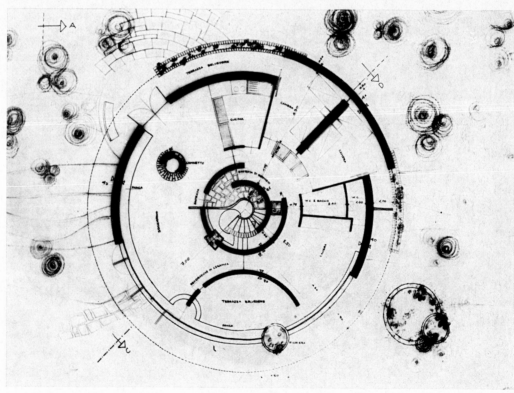

Marcello d'Olivo: Villa Mainardi at Lighano Pineta, Italy.
Top – general view. Bottom – floor plan of the residential floor

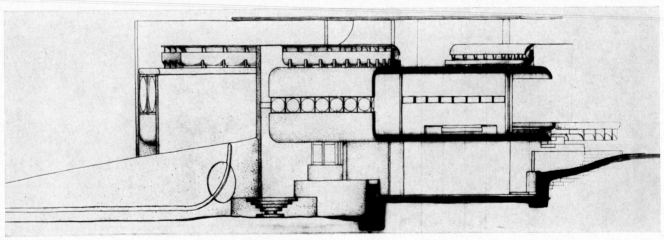

Marcello d'Olivo: Villa Spezzotti at Lighano Pineta, Italy. Terrace.

Left – general view and section

Affonso Eduardo Reidy: Week-end house at Itapaua, Brazil.
View from the southwest

Right – J. M. Martorell, Oriol Bohigas and David Mackay:
Dwelling house at Palau de Plegamans (Barcelona).
Bottom – floor plan

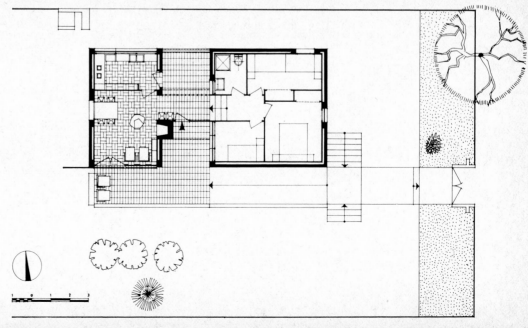

Arne Jacobsen: Dwelling house at Vedbaek, Denmark. Top –
general view. Bottom – courtyard side

Top – Elie Azagury: Dwelling house at Youssoufia, Morocco.

Bottom – Ralph Erskine: Dwelling house at Lidingö, Sweden.

Amancio d'Alpoim Quedes: Dwelling house in Lourenco
Marques, Mozambique.

Top – Christian Norberg-Schulz: Dwelling house at Porto Ercole, Italy.

Bottom – B. Knutsen: Single-family houses in Oslo

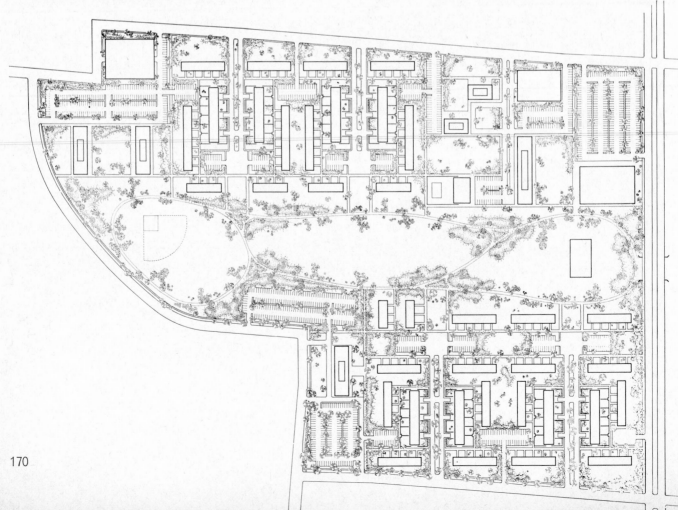

Ludwig Mies van der Rohe: Blocks of apartments and terraced houses in Detroit, Michigan.

Top left – terraced houses. Bottom – site plan

Harry Weese: Terraced houses in Chicago, Illinois

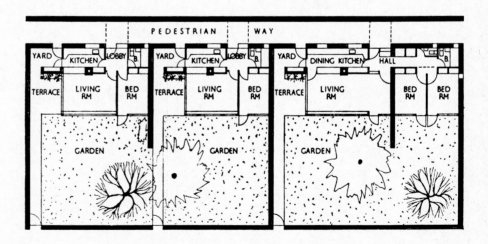

Powell and Moya: Dwelling houses for the employees of the Princess Margaret Hospital at Swindon, England. Bottom – floor plan

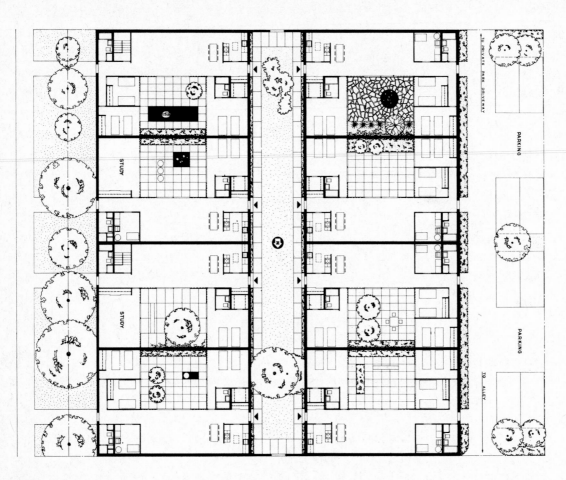

174

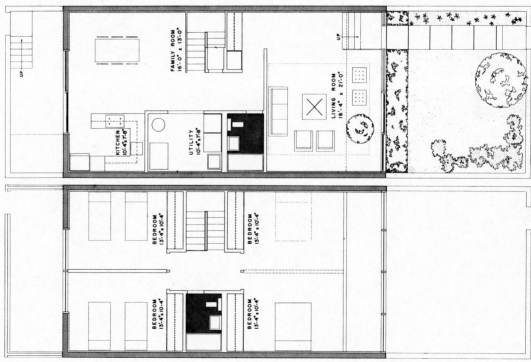

Y. C. Wong: Atrium houses in Chicago, Illinois. Bottom – floor plan.

Left – Y. C. Wong: Terraced houses in Kenwood, Chicago. Bottom – floor plans of the ground floor and first upper story

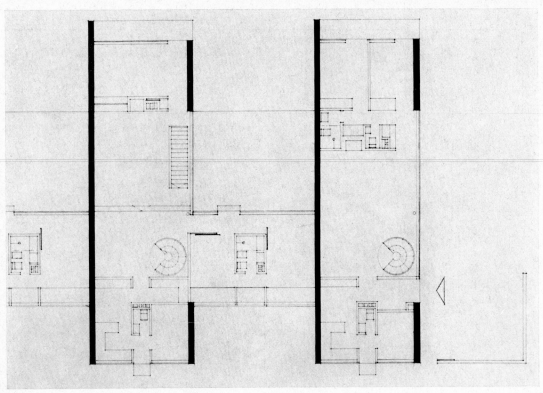

Kaija and Heikki Siren: Terraced houses in Tapiola, Finland.
Top – general view. Bottom – ground floor.

Right – individual house

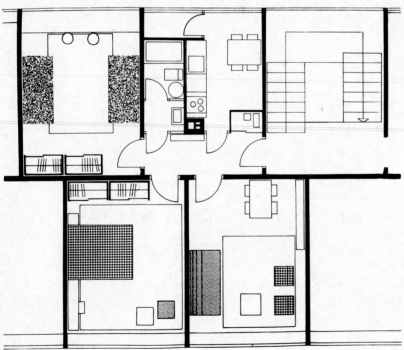

Zeljko Solar and Bogdan Budimirov: Residential block made of prefabricated units in Zagreb, Yougoslavia. Bottom – floor plan of an apartment.

Top – R. Braem: Prefabricated house in Antwerp.

Bottom – Roland Rainer: Prefabricated house in Vienna

Top – aerial view of Brasília.

Bottom – aerial view of Islamabad, Pakistan.

C. A. Doxiadis: Housing project in Baghdad.

Atelier 5: Halen Settlement near Berne, Switzerland. General view.

Top left – detail. Bottom – swimming pool

Top – Atelier 5: Halen Settlement near Berne – terrace

Bottom – Roland Frey, Hermann Schroder and Claus Schmidt: Competition design for the residential area of Stuttgart-Neugereut, Germany. Terrace of an apartment.
Right – "Residential Hill" (model).

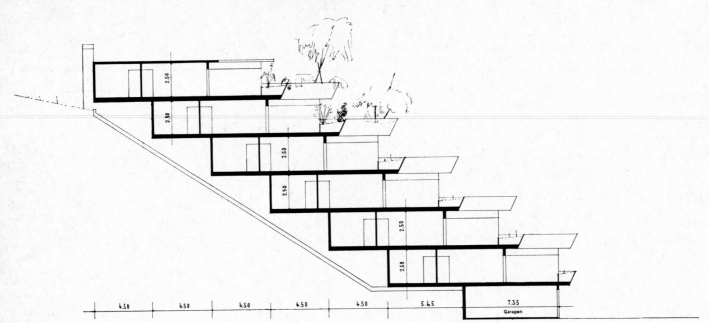

Fritz Stucky and Rudolf Meuli: Terrace apartments at Zug, Switzerland. Individual house with terrace.

Top left – general view. Bottom – section

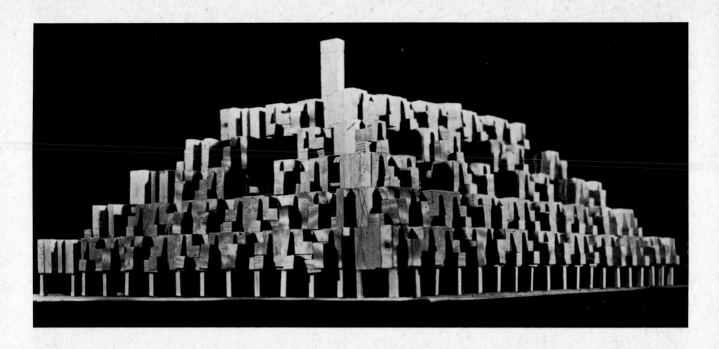

Top – Leopold Gerstel: Terrace building in Haifa, Israel (model).

Bottom – Moshe Safdie, David, Barott and Boulva: Habitat '67. Project for the Montreal World Fair (model).

188

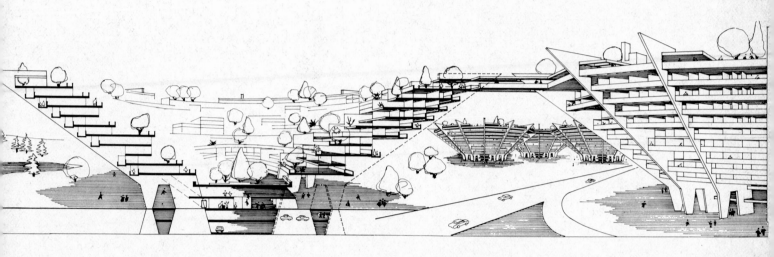

Top – Walter Jonas: Intra-settlement (project).

Bottom – Kenzo Tange: Terrace housing project (model).

189

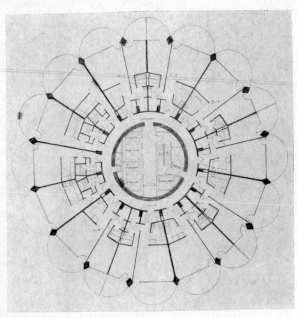

Bertrand Goldberg: Marina City in Chicago.
Top – detail. Bottom – plan of a typical residential floor.

Right – overall view

190

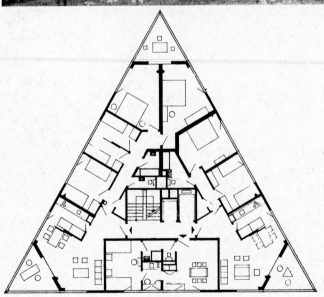
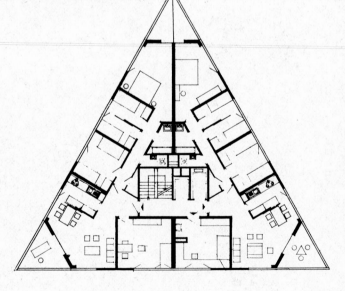

Fritz Stucky and Rudolf Meuli: Leimatt multi-storey buildings at Oberwil/Zug, Switzerland. Top – general view of whole group. Bottom – floor plans. Left – floor with 5½-, 2-, and 3½-room apartments. Right – Floor with 5½-, 1-, and 4½-room apartments. On the right page – individual house.

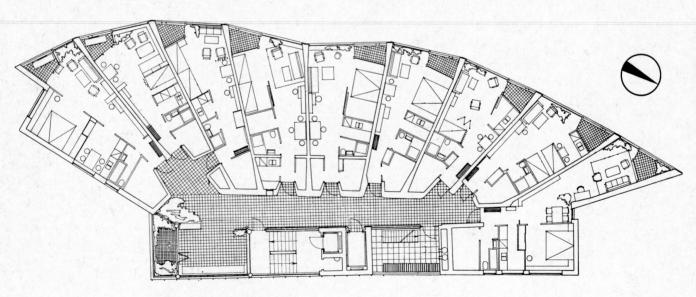

Alvar Aalto: Multi-story building in the Neue Vahr, Bremen.
Top – general view. Bottom – plan of a normal floor.

Right – View from the south

Top – Eric Cumine: Block of apartments in Hong Kong.
Bottom – Braem, de Mol and Moerkerke: Block of apartments
in Leuven, Belgium.

196

György Vedres: Dwelling house in Budapest

Al Mansfeld and Dora Gad: Apartment block in Haifa, Israel.

Top – V. Simionescu and D. Mihaila: Blocks of apartments in Bucharest.

Bottom – J. Klen, M. Jaralim, G. Kratochisl, E. Simek: Apartment blocks in Prague

Paul Romero and Fernando Salines: Dwelling house at Habana del Este, Cuba.

Top right – Tecton with Skinner, Bailey and Lubetkin: Housing project in London

Bottom – Kunio Mayekawa: Multi-story residential blocks in Tokyo.

Carlos Raúl Villanueva, Guido Bermudez, Carlos Brando and
Juan Centella: Housing project in Caracas

Palmer and Turner: Housing project in Kowloon, Hong Kong

Enrico Castiglioni, Cesare Casati, Enzo Hybsch and Antonio
Locati: Plan for the new center of Turin (model).

Left – Kenzo Tange: Plan for the extension of the city of Tokyo
(model).

Top – Yona Friedman: Plan for building over the city of Paris.

Bottom – Schulze-Fielitz and Friedman: Project for a bridge-
city over the English Channel (model)

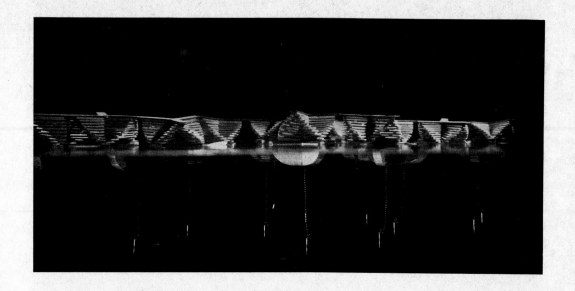

Top – Noriaki Kurokawa: Project for a floating city (model).

Bottom – Kiyonori Kikutake: Project for a tower city

Richard Buckminster Fuller: Roofing – in part of Manhattan
with a cupola having a diameter of 1.8 Miles (project)